# Unlocking
# the Will
# to Learn

For Jane and Emily,
teacher and learner

# Unlocking the Will to Learn

### Christine A. Johnston

**CORWIN PRESS, INC.**
A Sage Publications Company
Thousand Oaks, California

*For information address*:

Corwin Press, Inc.
A Sage Publications Company
2455 Teller Road
Thousand Oaks, California 91320
E-mail: order@corwin.sagepub.com

SAGE Publications Ltd.
6 Bonhill Street
London EC2A 4PU
United Kingdom

SAGE Publications India Pvt. Ltd.
M-32 Market
Greater Kailash I
New Delhi 110 048 India

Printed in the United States of America

**Library of Congress Cataloging-in-Publication Data**

Johnston, Christine A.
    Unlocking the will to learn / author, Christine A. Johnston.
        p.    cm.
    Includes bibliographical references and index.
    ISBN 0-8039-6437-4 (cloth: acid-free paper).—ISBN 0-8039-6392-0
(pbk.: acid-free paper)
    1. Learning.   2. Learning, Psychology of.   3. Teaching.
I. Title.
LB1060.J48   1996
    370.15′23—dc20                                                95-50206

This book is printed on acid-free paper.

99   10   9   8   7   6   5   4   3   2

Corwin Press Production Editor: Tricia K. Bennett
Corwin Press Typesetter: Andrea D. Swanson

# Contents

# Preface

During the summer of 1993, I was approached by a group of primary and secondary school teachers enrolled in graduate education courses at Rowan College of New Jersey. They were interested in more information about the research that I had recently completed concerning how students learn and don't learn. They were most interested in gaining a better understanding of how the natural way people do any type of task affects our learning behavior. They asked important questions: How can teachers know what learning behaviors a student possesses? How would this information change our perceptions of student behavior? What could we do with that knowledge? How would we teach differently? How would we physically structure our classes to accommodate students' learning behaviors?

The overwhelming consensus was that they did not want an instrument that needed to be "sent away" to be scored. They also did not want a numerical profile that required someone else's interpretation of their students' behavior. "Our students are tested to death. They cringe every time we place a bubble answer sheet in front of them." "Can't we come up with a way to gather this information that is both affordable and accessible for my district?"

Their second request was for information about interactive learning behaviors that they could use in their classrooms. "We need real-life scenarios." "We need to 'hear and see' these students. Can't you capture their typical behavior so we can identify with them?" "Won't someone give us practical ideas for what we can do and what we shouldn't be doing as teachers?" "We need a way to better understand the students we have." "We need teaching methods, not more testing."

From these conversations evolved a comprehensive strategy for getting to know a student's learning behaviors. The strategy consists of two parts: a user-friendly instrument and a softcover text. The instrument helps both the teacher and the student learn about their natural way of "doing" the task of learning. The text explains how both learners and teachers alike can use the Learning Combination process to unlock the will to learn and the will to teach.

# Acknowledgments

"Many different people contributed in many different ways to the writing of this book" is the standard line that begins most literary efforts. In the case of this book, not only is the line accurate, it is providential. Not only did many people support the writing of the text, but also they participated in its development through both "word and deed." I am grateful to those individuals who have allowed me to use personal anecdotes to amplify the message of this text.

I am especially grateful to the sequential, precise, technical, and confluent reviewers of the manuscript: Nancy Braack, Joanne Goodman, Donna Hallworth, Robin Herman, Sharon Hervold, Joanne Johnson, Robert Krastek, Mary Louise Lavery, Allison Nicholson, June Palmunen-Fisher, Greg Rohrman, Joanne Walsh, and Ann Woodworth.

Because this text is based on research conducted within the United States and abroad, I wish to acknowledge those who have contributed to the research component: John Johnston, Queens University, Belfast, Northern Ireland; Mary Hayes, Nottingham Trent University, Nottingham, United Kingdom; Lois Addy, Harrogate General Hospital, Harrogate, United Kingdom; Joseph Mifsud, University of Malta; Mark Borg, University of Malta, the Republic of Malta; and Joel Johnston, British American Security Information Council, Washington, D.C.

I also wish to acknowledge Mardi Lesher and Debra Neill, whose contributions to the project included hours of discussion and feedback. Clearly, this text would not exist without the faithful and steady hand of M. E. Westermaier, whose technical skills and discernment of the English language made the ideas behind the text a reality. Finally, I am indebted to Gary Dainton for his commitment to bringing this project to fruition.

# How to Use
# *Unlocking the Will to Learn*

### Read it to understand your own learning process.

Use the glosses to direct you to more extensive discussions of the topics presented. The teacher-scholar will find much to consider on the basis of the book's references to current research on cognitive science, brain science, learning styles, multiple intelligences, and self-regulated learning.

### Read it to understand your students' learning processes.

This book is written with the teacher-practitioner in mind. Literally tens of dozens of real-life examples fill the pages of this book. You will find your students among them!

### Read it as a practical hands-on guide for implementing interactive learning in your classroom.

This book spans everything from theoretical constructs to virtual "make-and-take" projects for classroom use. Each chapter brings with it more and more practical suggestions for teacher use including the Learning Combination Inventory, scoring key, and interpretation guide.

**Read it as a part of a staff development program.**

*Unlocking the Will to Learn* provides a central focus and beginning point for introducing effective learner-centered instructional practices, including how to group students for maximal effect for cooperative learning, how to apply interactive learning in all subject areas, and how to use the Interactive Learning Model to facilitate integrated curriculum-instruction.

# About the Author

**Christine A. Johnston** is Associate Professor of Educational Administration at Rowan College of New Jersey. She earned an Ed.D. in administration and supervision from Rutgers University, an M.A. in urban planning from the University of Wisconsin-Milwaukee, and a B.A. in secondary education from the University of Wisconsin-Eau Claire. Her career has been shaped by opportunities provided through a Ford Foundation Internship, a National Science Foundation Fellowship, and a New Jersey Governor's Teacher's Grant. Her professional life has spanned three decades of teaching, administration, collaboration, and research in public schools and government agencies. She has been especially successful in building local, national, and international partnerships that bridge the gap from conceptualization to practical application. A dedicated researcher and enthusiastic presenter, she has focused her concern on the nurturing of real schools, real students, and real educators through attention to effective communication, a clear understanding of the learning process, and a commitment to the student-centered classroom. She is the author of *Empowering the Organization Through Professional Talk* (1994).

# PART

# 1

# SETTING THE STAGE

## Before We Begin

Throughout this book, I use a number of metaphors. Metaphors do several things. They bring pieces of information together. They synthesize in a way that touches a number of our senses—visual, auditory, and tactile. Although those who report scientific research may only occasionally express their findings in these terms, I think that those of us who want to read and understand scholarly literature can gain helpful insights through the use of metaphors.

I don't wish to suggest that metaphors represent the totality of the point being made. My intention is not to have the reader dwell on the metaphor at the expense of the information I wish to impart. The message is the focus; the metaphor is the medium.

The metaphors I have chosen—*center stage, a combination lock, fabric, a rock, and a tool*—may also serve another purpose. You may want to use these same metaphors with your student-learners. This picture-language may help them understand the information that will assist them in developing an awareness of their will, their learning patterns, and their learning process.

But for now, all you need to be concerned with is turning the page. The stage is set. Enjoy *Unlocking the Will to Learn*.

# Chapter

# 1

Students belong at the center of educational outcomes.
—Levin, 1994, p. 759

# Setting the Stage for Unlocking the Will to Learn

You are sitting in an auditorium awaiting the beginning of the school play. You've read the playbill and have noted the key contributors to this effort: the playwright, the director, the set and costume designers, the stage and lighting directors, and the financial supporters. This is obviously going to be a wonderful production.

Just as you finish reading this information, the auditorium lights begin to dim, and the curtain rises. The audience gasps, and you nod in approval as the brilliance of the stage lights reveals a most enchanting set. This initial reaction is followed by a pregnant pause—just a brief pause—then an awkward pause. No one appears. The spotlight searches the stage, but no one appears. You check the playbill again. Good grief! There is no cast listed. Amid all your interest in the details of the production, you've failed to observe the absence of a cast. All is in readiness, but there will be no play. Why? Because those responsible for producing the school play have forgotten the most vital element, the central issue—the actors—the children—the students!

A bit dramatic? Rather silly? After all, who would forget the students? That is a very important question. It bears consideration as we set the stage to examine the issue of the learner within the school context. Who would forget the learner?

Here's one answer: A mid-Atlantic state's newly adopted certification requirements for the principalship use more than 10 pages to describe the topics, themes, and skills that a principal should possess. These include labor relations, school law, organizational theory, public relations, personnel management, and technology. Nowhere in the document is there reference to the learner! Nowhere in the document is the student mentioned. Nowhere in the document is either the teacher or the curriculum mentioned. Who would forget the learner? Sometimes even the best intentioned. In the theater of schooling today, the learner is frequently left in the wings behind debates over restructuring, outcome-based education, privatization, contracts, scheduling, and testing. Lost in the ballyhoo is the purpose of having an educational structure—the learner.

How did this happen? At the turn of the century, those responsible for developing the American educational system made the decision to emphasize the product of learning rather than the process of learning. Caught up in the "cult of efficiency" and the industrial model of cost-effectiveness, those developing the educational system chose to standardize schooling to mass-produce learners. They structured the school systems, standardized the learning environment, and scripted the curricula to do just that. As a consequence, teachers now contend with state-mandated subjects and state-mandated performance measures. This is the theater in which we work each day. The classroom is the stage on which this is played out. But where is the student in all of this? Where is the learner?

Callahan, 1962

We all learned the answer to the purpose of education in our pedagogy classes. The answer then and the answer now is the student, the learner. The learner is the reason for the school to exist. Here, read the words once again:

Whitehead, 1929, p. 17

**The central task of education is the . . . successful dealing with human minds.**

Bruner, 1960, p. 9

**The purpose of schooling is to help each student achieve his/her optimum intellectual development.**

The message of those courses remains quite clear: Don't forget the child. Don't forget what teachers are all about—the learner and the process of learning. Now, more than ever, it is important to remember this: To be a teacher means to make a lifelong commitment to keeping the learner central to the teaching-learning process.

**To be a teacher means to make a lifelong commitment to keeping the learner central to the teaching-learning process.**

The message is eminently clear. The cast has been chosen. The title of the production is struck. The lead role in education belongs to the learner—the student! Make no mistake about who is cast in the leading role. It is the learner. The learner is center stage, surrounded by a host of supporting cast including parents and teachers. No building, no curriculum, no organizational structure, and no technology can remove the centrality of the learner in this production.

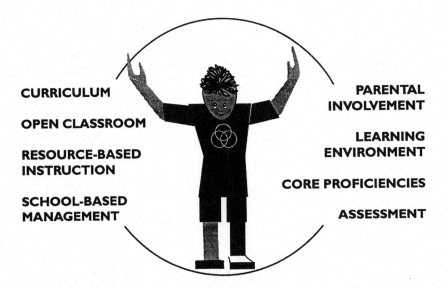

**CURRICULUM**

**OPEN CLASSROOM**

**RESOURCE-BASED INSTRUCTION**

**SCHOOL-BASED MANAGEMENT**

**PARENTAL INVOLVEMENT**

**LEARNING ENVIRONMENT**

**CORE PROFICIENCIES**

**ASSESSMENT**

**Figure 1.1.**

True, the successful operation of a school requires good leadership and a professional staff. It also requires effective planning and management. Central to all these individuals and activities, however, is the learner. It is the learner who is center stage. This book is based on that premise. It focuses on how to unlock and what unlocks the learner's motivation to learn.

The reader is hereby notified of casting calls for the real-life drama titled *Unlocking the Will to Learn.* Only student-learners and teacher-learners need apply!

2

Schooling will succeed when
knowledge is not force fed to
children, but rather children are
encouraged to construct their
own ways of representing
knowledge.
—Santrouck, 1994, p. 243

# Critical Elements

*The Learner, the Teacher,
and the Learning Process*

## The Learner

I can still see David Lund, his eyes red from crying, his nose dripping. I remember thinking, "What's wrong? Nobody's hit you. Stop crying. Let go of your mother's leg!" The teacher talked to David; David's mother talked to David. David would not be consoled. He did not want to be in school, and that was that. My mother said he was an only child, a momma's boy. He was "tied to his mother's apron strings." I thought that was odd because I hadn't seen any apron wrapped around him. All I saw was a very upset 6-year-old.

On the other hand, I wasn't upset. I was ready. Of course, my big brother, Bob, had made certain of that. He had told me what to say and what not to say. He told me all about Mrs. Curry, my first-grade teacher, and I knew all the signs of when she was pleased and when she wasn't. The only thing he had not prepared me for was her right arm. There was a large, craterlike indentation in her bicep. I wanted very much to ask her what had caused it, but I didn't because Bob had told me, "Let Mrs. Curry do the talking." (I later learned that Mrs. Curry had had a smallpox vaccination which "didn't take." I thought that was an inaccurate description because it had "taken" a good part of her arm.)

Bob had also warned me that if things got out of hand and Mrs. Curry raised her voice, the best thing to do was to crawl under the desk and wait for things to settle down. Well, you can't believe everything a big brother says. The first time I evacuated my chair and found cover under the desk, I was greeted with, "Christine. What are you doing? Lost something or looking for loose change?" I was humiliated. So much for sibling advice.

Even now as I reflect on my first days of school, I see that my level of concreteness was high and my level of abstraction was limited. I was a literalist. I had memory; I was familiar with the sounds of many words, but I did not have the ability to understand and discern the intent or message of them. I took them at face value. I was a typical 6-year-old. And like most 6-year-olds, I was very impressionable. I aimed to please; I wanted to be liked; I wanted what I did to meet the teacher's and my parents' approval. All of this is typical of the young child new to school and new to formalized learning.

I did, however, have a real advantage over David because I had someone who had given me clues about what to expect and how to conduct myself as a first grader. I did not have to find out these things for myself. My brother had paved the way by easing my mind and explaining to me the drill of a typical school day as well as the role I was to play as a student. He made clear the teacher's expectation of performance long before I arrived at the schoolhouse door. David, on the other hand, was not prepared.

Why am I telling all of this? Because I believe it is essential for each of us to recognize that the students come to us in September with all types of ideas, expectations, hopes, and misconceptions about the teacher, the classroom, the learning that is to take place, and, yes, even themselves. It is foolish to believe that the child arrives ready to receive instruction, internalize information, apply it, and demonstrate how to use it in a manner and to a degree that the teacher, district, and the state have deemed achievement. The groundwork for becoming a student-learner must be laid first.

This is particularly true in the primary grades. The data bank of experiences of a first grader is much smaller than that of a fifth- or eighth-grade student. For the most part, the child new to "schooling" needs to develop the socialization skills of how to behave in a classroom; how and when to talk; and how to take information, remember it, and use it at the appropriate time. For many, this is considered learning. For those who understand the learning process, these conforming behaviors are seen as schooling, not learning. But that topic will be taken up shortly.

Suffice it to say that the children who come into a school setting do so with a mixture of limited schooling experiences and unclear expectations about what will take place. They are bewildered about how they fit into the entire situation. For these children, the words *student* and *learner* are new. How they relate to each other may remain a mystery to the child for some time. Or, as we are reminded each time we read about dropouts or the disaffected school population, some children never connect these terms even after 12 years of schooling.

## The Teacher

I remember my first day of teaching as well as I remember my first day of school. I faced 23 tenth graders who were enrolled in a course titled "Business English." They had been schooled well. This was the first day of the new school year, so they sat in their rows facing forward waiting to see what I was all about. Not that they were enthusiastic— they were just there, and they were quiet.

I, on the other hand, was a mixture of composure on the outside and turmoil on the inside. Who were these people, and whatever was I supposed to do with them? I looked at the roster of names. I couldn't even read them! Tschaswicz. Benasheski. Tesch. As I stood facing them, the point of all the endless course work, methods classes, and practicums in which I had engaged turned to vapor in my memory bank. All was replaced by the single thought, "Now what? What am I going to do to keep them busy for 55 minutes? What do I know that they don't? What do I know that they need?"

The questions all centered around what I (mistakenly) thought teaching was about—me, the teacher. So what did I do? I did what most first-year teachers do. I abandoned my textbook knowledge and headed straight for my experiences. I grabbed on to the memories of what my teachers had done—how they had taught me. I took a deep breath and announced, "Welcome to Business English. I am Ms. Dicke. I will get to know your names within a few days, but for right now, please open your notebooks and let's begin by having you write down the rules of the classroom."

Like most new teachers and even some seasoned teachers, my fall-back position was to resort to what was most familiar, what was most ingrained in me—the patterns of teaching I had experienced during my 18 years as a student in public and postsecondary education. That was my comfort zone. I knew that territory well. What I did not know was that I had focused on the wrong issue. It would take me 5 more years of "teaching" before I learned what student-centered learning was about.

The primary insight to be gained from this anecdote is that we teach as we were taught.

One of the reasons it is difficult to put the learner center stage is that teachers have been center stage during our entire schooling experience. Consequently, once we become teachers, we perpetuate this system without examining its shortcomings. As one graduate of the educational system reflected, "Teachers have an almost blind faith in the system because they are products of that system." The point is that before the teacher became a teacher, the teacher was a student. After 16-plus years as a student interacting with a cast of tens of teachers, each student has developed his or her own script of "How to Be a Teacher." We can all remember the ones we most admired and wished to emulate. We can also remember the ones who left an indelible mark, a mark that in my case caused me to pledge silently that should I ever teach a student as I had been taught by these persons, "may my chalk turn to dust and I be assigned to cafeteria duty in perpetuity."

**We teach as we were taught.**

Why such a heady remark? I believe the role of the teacher is based on a sacred trust, premised on the teacher's commitment to

Unfortunately, instead of upholding that trust, teachers too frequently replace learning with schooling. They take their own school experiences, add what they have learned in college courses and clinical experiences, and use the result to acclimate the incoming student to school. In doing so, the teacher assumes the role of architect and constructor of the child's school experiences. The teacher explains what the expectations are in the classroom, the hallway, the bathrooms, the cafeteria, and the playground. The teacher is on the front line of the socialization process of the learner. Many others contribute to this process, but for the first 2 or 3 years of schooling, it is primarily the teacher who shapes, refines, and hones the child's learning behaviors into the academic performance of a student.

The student-learner goes through this process each time she or he enters a new learning environment: a new classroom, a new building, a new grade. Whether entering elementary, middle, or high school, the student is required to focus on acclimation and adjustment to the demands of schooling. Frequently missing from the schooling process, however, is attention to the child's individual learning process.

## The Learner and the Teacher

The assumption most widely held by teachers is that children entering the school system are there to learn to be good students; that is, they are prepared to internalize the information and apply it to various situations to demonstrate that they understand and know how to use the information on a standardized test. When we develop our learning environment around this premise, we simply fail to see the difference between the processes of schooling and learning. We fail to separate the schooling-socialization process from the individual's unique learning process.

| A Child's Learning Adventure | | | |
| --- | --- | --- | --- |
| **Key Concerns of the Teacher About the Student** | | | |
| Induction | Socialization | Standardization | Critical Juncture |
| **Key Actions of the Learner** | | | |
| Age 4-5 Enters school; assessed on readiness, ability to separate, health, and wellness | Age 6-8 Develops standard behaviors through socialization into the formal organization of schooling; seeks to receive approval for performance | Age 9-10 Is aware of self and what the teacher expects for performance; is becoming aware that what he or she wants to do and what the teacher expects are very different | Age 11-12 Determines that performance is acceptable or unacceptable; opts to buy into school or to drop out |
| **Key Concerns of the Learner** | | | |
| Who am I outside my world of home? How am I to act? What can I do to please? | Who am I to the teacher? How am I to please? Who am I to please? | Who am I as a student in the classroom? How can I be me? What if I can't please? | Who am I to my peers? How can I fit in? What do I care if I please? |

**Box 2.1.**

I teach first grade, and even at the beginning of a child's education, empowering a child to feel ownership for his or her learning can make all the difference in how that child views what it means to learn.
—Falkowski, 1995[1]

If we study the difference, we recognize that *schooling* is formally training persons how to conduct themselves in the place called school. *Learning,* that is, the process of learning, is a highly personal process whereby individuals use their informed, engaged, and reflective effort to develop their abilities to know, do, and feel. As you can see, teaching children to be learners involves more than standardizing their behaviors!

"A Child's Learning Adventure" (see Box 2.1) represents this difference by juxtaposing the stages of schooling (induction, socialization, standardization, and critical juncture) against the child's developmental concerns as a learner. Notice the progression of the learner's development. Take special notice of the questions that are directing the learner's sense of self. It is obvious that the manner in which the learner-teacher-school socialization process occurs strongly influences the learner's perception of self. If the match between the learner's school behavior and the teacher's school expectations is good, the new learner develops a positive sense of self, an "I can do" attitude.

If, on the other hand, the learner recognizes that the manner in which he or she learns is different from what the teacher expects, the learner begins to question his or her worth as a student. The learner's self-worth diminishes and confusion ensues. If this continues unnoticed or unaddressed, the child's learning curve takes a tumble. Patterns of school behavior appear that are not appropriate, acceptable, or tolerable. All interest on the part of the student wanes. Attention and motivation become areas of concern for the teacher and eventually the parent. The learner's sense of "who I am" in the classroom is in turmoil. The teacher-student connection is in jeopardy; the schooling-learning connection is in peril.

At issue here are two agendas: the teacher's agenda to "school" the child and develop a student and the child's agenda to thrive in the school environment and learn about the world around him or her. The child can easily become confused by the expectation of the first and the desires of the second. Take David and Christine, for instance. Christine came to school filled with expectations about the teacher and the routine. She was prepared to adjust to school and to get on with learning. She had a strong sense of self as an individual and as a learner. David, on the other hand, was more vulnerable from the outset. He did not want to be there. He did not want to be *schooled*. If during his first years, David reached the point where he felt he did not fit in, or could not learn, then his sense of self as a student and as a learner would falter. This scenario is played out over and over again, classroom after classroom.

When the children lose confidence in themselves, that loss spirals into a diminished sense of self-worth. They ask inside themselves in quiet, worried voices, "Why don't I fit?" This soon becomes, "How can I fit?" Finally, the question changes to a statement, "I don't care if I fit."

The first indicators show in the learner's lack of attention and investment in learning in the classroom. This is soon broadcast through the standard document of record, the report card. "Bright but not working up to capacity." "Fails to use study time wisely." "Frequently off-task." "Daydreams." "Unprepared for class." "Does not complete homework in a timely fashion." "Unmotivated." "Conference requested."

Then begin the choral responses of teachers and parents, "He seems so bright." "No matter what I say, I can't get him to do his schoolwork." "She was always such a good student. She had all S's until fourth grade, and now she doesn't seem to care anymore."

| Kindergarten | Second Grade | Fourth Grade | Sixth Grade |
|---|---|---|---|
| ☑ Daydreams | ☑ Bright; not working to level | ☑ Does not complete homework | ☑ Fails to use study time well |
| ☑ Off-task | ☑ Unprepared | ☑ Unmotivated | ☑ Conference |

The mixed agendas of schooling versus learning contribute to the child's feeling that "I am not capable." "I am not capable of doing my work. I am not capable of demonstrating my knowledge. I am not capable of doing my work in a way that is acceptable to my teacher." As a result of this conflict, the child is confused and begins to struggle with the question: To please the teacher or not to please the teacher?

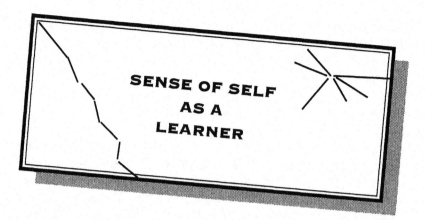

**Figure 2.1.**

Satir, 1972

To give in to the demands of schooling (which the child is now beginning to think are the same as learning) or to stand alone against a fine-tuned schooling machine? To admit "I am not capable of being a learner in this school environment" or to rebel and ignore the threats of teachers and parents alike? The frustration and trauma resulting from making this choice are very real. With either choice, the child's self-esteem is seriously damaged. That damage can carry with it a lifelong effect.

When the learner chooses to please the teacher and fit into the process of schools, the child begins to operate with great deliberateness and under much stress. The sense of what is not pleasing quickly shifts from "my schoolwork is not pleasing to the teacher" to "I am not pleasing to the teacher." Now the child must decide to shift from developing skills as a learner to developing the skills of pleasing the teacher.

My teacher knows how much I know and that makes me feel good. I have my technique and she likes it and I use it.
—Age 6

*Learning early to please the teacher*

The desire to please others is an intense drive within each of us. We want to please those in authority over us because we want to survive. We want to please because we hope if we please the teacher and our parents enough, we survive and possibly thrive. The hope is "If I can please this individual who is central to my life, if I can meet this person's expectations to the degree that this person has set, then I am acceptable. I can be liked, and I can be loved. And that is what I am seeking. I want that sense of acceptance given to me by those whom I respect or see as important in my life."

Duncan, 1991

It does not take much prompting for children to sense that they need to demonstrate knowledge or work in a manner different from their current mode of performance. For an elementary student, it is painful to come to the recognition that "the way in which I am doing my schoolwork or the way in which I think about things" is not what the teacher expects, respects, or values.

Vygotsky, 1962

But for many, this change in learning behavior is a long stretch—especially when inside they are saying, "I don't see it in the same way; it doesn't come together for me in the same way. The information isn't processing in the same way. I don't value information or the specifics of information to the same degree." "I don't see the organization; I don't see the logic; I don't see a natural progression." "I don't understand how these things work; I don't see why I have to work with others." "I can't think of anything to do; I can't come up with ideas like others."

To change or adapt one's natural process of learning is difficult. As a result, many simply choose to opt out of the school program. Oh, physically they remain, at least until 9th or 10th grade, but mentally they abandon their interest or drive to succeed by the 5th grade. These students are now warehoused, as one student described it, "within these four white cinder block walls with kiddies pictures on them." "Me, how would I learn? I would go home. I would learn there. I would come back once in a while and see my friends. I just don't see any reason to sit here doing rows and rows of math problems or writing about what I did last summer. I've got better things to be doing."

When we first observe these student behaviors, we think, "The child just needs to mature." And the child thinks, "If I just keep trying, I will get better at doing this." The message "try harder" is a little voice within us that says, "If I at least go through the motions, look like the person sitting next to me, mimic that behavior, then maybe answers will come to me in the same way as they do to that person . . . maybe reading will come to me in the same way . . . maybe . . . maybe . . ."—when, in fact, going through the motions is not an authentic learning activity even if it is acceptable school behavior.

For learners to succeed, they must do more than be "try hard" students. They must put forth measurable effort that results in successful performance. For example, if the learners are asked to prioritize information, manipulate information, and retain information, then the learners need to engage the mental processes that will achieve this. If such a learning process is truly foreign to the students, then simply trying harder won't make a difference. Repeatedly doing something unsuccessfully can only increase frustration and lower self-esteem.

At this point the issue of schooling versus learning looms even greater. The teacher observes the learner's behavior and responds with "hurry up." "You are falling behind. You are holding us back. You aren't developing at the same speed that I need to have you develop. You aren't performing at the same rate as you are supposed to. I have school achievement standards to meet. How am I going to address this? I have 22 other students. At least 15 of the 22 are moving along at a certain rate. They are responding to the learning process as it is presented in this classroom. What's happening here? It can't be me. I hope it's not me. I'm certain it can't be me because the other 15 are doing so well. It must be the child."

And the child feels the underlying "hurry up" message of schooling and responds with "I'm trying as hard as I can." All of this creates an emotional turmoil that causes the learner to lose the will or drive to learn because the learner doesn't feel any success or any purpose or relevance in either the process or the content of what he or she is required to learn.

Kahler, 1977

Johnston, 1994a

Dear Mrs. P.,
Why must I awlways wate for drechsons. Just let me start. If I need help I will ask for it. Please. No more drechsons!
—Age 8

*When "my" way doesn't match the teacher's*

Elkind, 1981

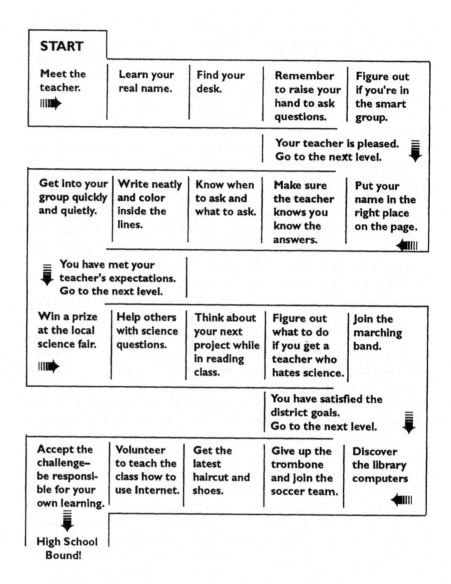

**Figure 2.2.** The Child's Learning Adventure Game

The teacher also loses the sense of achievement. "I'm not getting through. What could I be doing differently? Why isn't the student responding? Why am I feeling this distance?" The frustration for both learner and teacher mounts. The teacher sees the learner as a problem student in the classroom: withdrawn, uncooperative, unresponsive to instruction, difficult, and not performing up to grade-level standards. Unless this frustration is resolved, what follows quite naturally are the standard actions of the schooling process: referral, testing, classifying, and labeling.

This is an unhealthy experience for both the learner and the teacher. How did it begin? It began by losing sight of the learner and the learning process. It began when schooling replaced learning as the purpose for the child's presence in school. It continued by defining the learning process in a narrow manner.

## Note

1. From unpublished reflective journal entry. Reprinted by permission of Cindy Falkowski.

Every human being constitutes
a unique combination of
countless and differing factors.
—Allport, 1961, p. 354

# The Learning Process

*What's It All About?*

## The Traditional Approach

The learning process around which school has been developed is based on the belief that all learning occurs as a part of a child's use of his or her intelligence. The greater the intelligence, the more a child can learn. (Notice that no one says the more a child *will* learn because the latter is not true.) Intelligence for decades has been measured by examining a child's cognitive processes (information input, manipulation of information, and information output). It is believed that these cognitive processes equal the child's intelligence or innate aptitude for learning. The learner's level of cognition is most commonly measured by the child's performance on normed tests of reading comprehension, recall of information, formulation of thought, mathematical computation, and problem solving.

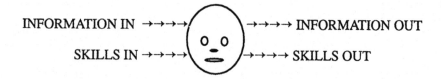

This model of the learning process is based on the degree of efficiency that learners exhibit as they gather information, retain information, and retrieve information at a given time and in a given format. We measure our learners on this model and gauge their readiness to participate in schooling on the basis of the outcomes. We structure the learning environment and teach our learners on the basis of this model. We develop yearlong programs of instruction, grade levels, and even buildings on the basis of this model, believing that we can put information into a child, pat it down, make room for the next dose, and move the child along the assembly line of learning.

I once worked as a culler in a glass factory. I stood at the end of a lehr, examining the glassware by hand before packaging it into a cardboard box and sending it down the line for a second inspection. There a person inspected my work and passed it along to the next step in the shipping process. Sometimes, late into the shift, when I was beginning to get worn out, and rows upon rows of glasses were still coming at me, I would panic. How could I adequately pick up six at a time, inspect them, and load them before the next row arrived! My answer, "Just pack them. Don't worry about a defect."

A *lehr* is a long conveyor belt that carries glassware from the annealing ovens to the quality control checkers.

When I was really creative, I tossed the three in my right hand and packed the three from my left. Either way, I was violating quality control standards. Eventually, I would hear from my supervisor, who would point out my outrageously high rate of "discards" or my lack of productivity. I was told to stick to the procedures. Keep my efficiency up and my creative culling down! And above all else, do it quickly and perfectly to please the supervisor.

The strength of this analogy lies in its representations of teachers whose classrooms are filled with rows upon rows of children who pass in and out of the doorway five or six times a day—students whom the teacher must cull, package, and move along to the next grade level all sorted and stamped with approval. The one new twist is that teachers are not only to inspect and detect but also to fill the glasses before moving them along to the next step in the processing. The entire educational program is based on this linear model of learning and the assembly line model of production.

When we treat the learning process as "information in—information out; skills in—skills out; problems in—problems out," we denigrate the wonderful process of learning. We reduce it to a cause-effect linear, rational model—which it isn't. Why then do we do it? One reason is that our lehrs are full, and the learners are coming down the line day in and day out. We do it because it is easier to handle that way. It is easier to do a standard procedure for all than to examine each. We use the assembly line approach to place primary knowledge and fundamental important basic skills into learners. If the learners do not respond within the prescribed time, we say, "You're not doing this well enough, fast enough, and complete enough to meet our standards." So we label and hold back children because they aren't ready to move to the next grade.

The assembly line schooling fails to recognize that learning is an individualized process. It ignores what we know about learning behaviors.

For example, we know we learn in bits and pieces. We have gestalts, epiphanies, and bits of brilliancies—not "turn a page, do a set of problems, now I know it." Rather, our mental processes operate in a wonderful turmoil of stirring, mixing, lumping, turning, twisting, revolving, spinning, gyrating, exploding, reforming, and constantly, constantly, interacting. We retain, we discard, we elevate, we cherish, and we ponder all that enters our mental processing system. We bag it, we examine it, we store it, we compare it, we judge it, we take it apart, we play with it. This is definitely not a linear model!

To think of learning in this manner means we are willing to reexamine our thoughts about how learning occurs. Such rethinking challenges us to come to grips with the difference between the processes of schooling and learning. It requires us to separate the schooling-socialization process from the individual's unique learning process.

Teaching standardization rather than learning has resulted in less than successful outcomes. We have only to look at our own families and our own classrooms to see this. Frequently, instead of a thriving learner, we find a child or young adult who "seems so bright" but just isn't "working up to potential." Our solution has been to counsel, cajole, poke, prod, teach study skills, issue detentions, retain, and remove social privileges to make the child a *good student*. We are failing, however, to assist the child in being a *successful learner*.

Reexamining our understanding of the learning process can open for us another way to address this critical juncture between children's schooling experiences and learning experiences. If our concern for the learners and for ourselves as teachers is high enough, then we are ready to intervene to remove the detractors of convenience, efficiency, and mass production from schooling. It marks our commitment to returning the learners to center stage. It is a good place to begin.

4

If a man does not keep pace with his companions, perhaps it is because he hears a different drummer. Let him step to the music which he hears, however measured, or far away.
—Thoreau, 1963, p. 246

# Illuminating the Process of Learning

## The Learning Process Revisited

The question of how a child learns is ageless. The topic is only slightly less daunting than how many angels can dance on the head of a pin and which came first, the chicken or the egg. For the teacher, however, the answer to the question of how a child learns is not just a matter of philosophical gymnastics. It is central to the issue of who the learner is.

Seeking to find a solid explanation of how humans learn is not a recent phenomenon. It has gone on for centuries. So why do I think we now have a better mousetrap or the definitive answer to all of this? I don't. Even as I forge ahead with these pages of the manuscript, the words of P. D. James, my favorite mystery novelist, loom ever present: No one has an identikit to the human mind.

Who could argue with that? The lack of an identikit, however, certainly has not prevented us from seeking answers to understanding how a child learns. The force that continues to drive our inquiry into the learning process is the learner-centered query, "What have we missed or failed to understand about how a child learns? What can help us as teachers be better facilitators of the child's learning process?"

Considering the amount of thought, conjecture, and experimentation that has accumulated through the centuries on this subject, where can we even begin to find the answer to these questions? I decided to

An *identikit* in a P. D. James novel such as *Shroud for a Nightingale* (1988, p. 154) is the apparatus used by forensics to gather evidence in a murder case.

**No one has an identikit to the human mind.**

begin by examining what we already know. To guide my inquiry, I developed a set of questions:

Brophy, 1987

- What mental processes are involved in the learning process?
- What is the explanation of how these work?
- What is motivation and how does it affect the learning process?

Having set the agenda of my inquiry, I began to examine the hundreds upon hundreds of pages, passages, and paradigms that have been developed in the quest to understand the mechanism and mechanics of learning. As I paged my way through the literature and studies, I found myself overwhelmed by the plethora of explanations complicated by different uses of the same terminology. I began to chart the key phrases and terms and to note the consistency or inconsistency of their use.

To keep me from slipping from the focus of who the learner is in real life and what learning looks like in the classroom, I decided to develop a more specific set of questions against which to consider the various explanations of the learning process. I used such basic questions as these:

- Does this explanation make sense? Is it well reasoned and logical?
- Does it take into consideration the whole child? The whole learner?
- Does it resolve our own questions about how we, ourselves, learn?
- Does it describe the learning behaviors of the children with whom we work?
- Do the models of the learning process address or explain intrinsic motivation?
- Does the explanation place an additional burden on me, the teacher, or does it suggest how the learner assumes responsibility for learning?

## Thoughts After Revisiting the Process

The single overriding conclusion of my investigation is that P. D. James was correct! There is no identikit to the human mind. The second conclusion I am willing to draw is that we learn using more than one mental faculty. The *triune brain,* the *trilogy of the mind,* and *interactive mental processes* have historically dominated the psychological literature, brain science, and, to some degree, the work of learning theorists. This should come as no surprise because references to the tripartite composition of the mind can be found in the earliest of Western literature.

Hilgard, 1980

Lattimore, 1965, p. 256

In the *Odyssey,* for example, Homer describes the protagonist, Odysseus, as contemplating his choices and determining "within the division of his mind" what action he will take when confronted with a predicament of epic proportions. Philosophers, psychologists, and educational practitioners all have devoted extensive energy to exploring the interworkings of the mind. Yet it has taken centuries for an empirically established theory of how the human mind functions to evolve.

Among the intrepid individuals who have offered their explanations are historic figures such as Plato and Kant and more recent names such as James, MacLean, and Snow. What differentiates these philosophers and psychologists from others who have explored the complexities of the human mind is that these individuals base their explanations on this assumption: The human essence consists of a tripartite configuration: the cognitive, the affective, and the conative.

**The human essence consists of a tripartite configuration: the cognitive, the affective, and the conative.**

For more than a half century in the field of education, the work of Piaget, Jung, and Skinner has formed the basis of our learning constructs. Although both Jung and Piaget refer to three functions or processing mechanisms of the mind, they did not elaborate on them to the extent and degree that these constructs became a noted part of their work.

Piaget, 1952
Jung, 1923
Flavell, 1980
Skinner, 1989

More recently, cognitive psychologists have shown a renewed interest in the tripartite theory. Their writings, and those that have focused on brain-based learning, hemisphericity, and motivation, suggest that Jung and Piaget may have failed to explore the interconnectedness of the brain. As we seek to understand better the trilogy of the mind and its effects on the learning process, each aspect of the tripartite theory of the mind (feelings, thoughts, and behavior) bears consideration as an important factor of the learning process.

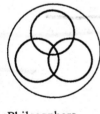

|  | **Divisions of the Mind From the Perspective of** |  |
|---|---|---|
| Philosophers | Three horses pulling the psychological chariot: feelings, thoughts, and behaviors; the trilogy of the mind consisting of thinking, feeling, and willing | Plato, cited in Keefe, 1992<br><br>Kant, 1888 |
| Psychologists | The complex of elements in an individual that feels, perceives, thinks, wills, and reasons | Jung, 1923 |
| Cognitive psychologists | A historically well-founded distinction between cognition, conation, and affectation; a matter of emphasis rather that partition; all learning involving some mixture of all three aspects | Snow & Jackson, 1992 |
| Learning style theorists | The composite of characteristics—cognitive, affective, and physiological factors—that serve as relatively stable indicators of how a learner perceives, interacts with, and responds to a learner's learning environment | Keefe & Languis, 1983 |
| Brain-based learning researchers | The triune brain encompassing the capacity and elegance of the way the brain learns | MacLean, 1978 |

**Box 4.1.**

## Cognition

**Intelligences
Abstraction
Experiences**

Intentionality connects knowing with doing.
—William James in May, 1969, p. 231

Cognition is our information processor. It is our mechanism for memorization. Our cognition is our language and communication center. It entertains communication of various configurations: musical notes; mathematical signs; artistic design; and physical contact between tool, object, and artisan. Cognition includes our experiences.

Cognition is the primary focus of public schooling. It certainly is key to having a child succeed in schooling. It is what we teach to; it is what we draw on when assessing learning. It has held sway in our educational learning paradigm—often to the detriment of the learner. Why? Because as we study the concept of the triune brain, we learn there is more to learning than cognitive processing.

## Conation

**Natural Skills
Pace
Autonomy**

There is also a close inner relationship between intentionality and caring. To "attend to" is at the very heart of the word and the relationship.
—William James in May, 1969, p. 228

Ferrell, 1983, p. 33

Hershberger, 1989

Leibniz, cited in Assagioli, 1973, p. 236

Snow & Jackson, 1992, p. 1

There is also the conative part of our learning process. Conation has been given a variety of names, including "purposeful striving," "persistence," and "the behavioral action." Those working in brain-based learning trace conation to the earliest development of the human brain, likening it to one of three brothers. They suggest the conative portion of the brain has evolved from the Reptilian Complex, the brain stem and mechanism that established the most basic of human functions, including territoriality, fight or flight, and ritualism. (This is not an unknown quantity to anyone who has had playground duty!) It is the action-behavior center. These same persons refer to it as the individual's bridge between the cognitive and affective aspects of the learning process.

Some learning style theorists term this second factor the *physiological* component. They do not define it, however, beyond "an environmental factor influencing a child's learning process." Still other researchers provide a number of broad-based descriptive categories of conative behaviors such as tempo, autonomy, level of energy, intention, and means of instigating action.

Cognitive psychologists have labeled conation the volitional factor. Well-known educational psychologists described conation as "among the most interesting and potentially useful psychological constructs which go beyond the conventional constructs of cognitive aptitude and achievement," suggesting that it is a part of "all human behavior, especially school learning and achievement."

## Affectation

**Feelings
Values
Sense of Self**

Affectation is the third member of the trilogy of the mind. Although affectation has achieved much recognition in the literature of learning, it has not achieved the same status in importance. Philosophers of ancient times termed affectation the soul, the heart, or the personality.

In modern times, the personality has been defined by the work of Myers and Briggs. The influence of their description of the affective has carried over into education and currently plays a prominent role in many explanations of learning styles. Learning style theorists rely heavily on the constructs of the Myers-Briggs Personality Inventory for their categorization of student learning styles. They depict learning styles on the basis of two axes: affectation and cognition or personality and aptitude.

Educational and cognitive psychologists describe the affective as a student's self-esteem and self-efficacy. Much of their literature is devoted to explaining how affectation, that is, what the learner values and how the learner perceives his or her capacity to learn, affects the learner's motivation to learn.

Self-concept cannot be divorced from learning.
—Caine & Caine, 1991, p. 127

Keefe & Ferrell, 1990

Myers-Briggs Type Indicator (Myers & Briggs, 1976)

Kuhl, 1986

**THE GENESIS**

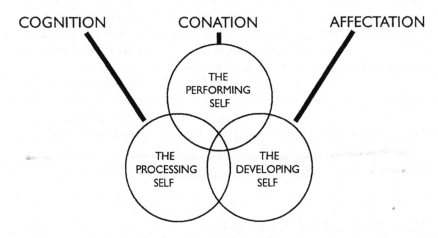

Figure 4.1.  The Synthesis of Components of the Mind

## How Do These Components Function With One Another?

Philosophers referred to cognition, conation, and affectation as the three horses of the psychological chariot. Alexander Graham Bell referred to the interaction as a focused energy of the affective, conative, cognitive connection when it moves into operation. Paul MacLean, former director of the Laboratory of the Brain and Behavior at the National Institute of Mental Health, refers to these constructs as the "Brothers Triune." All preach the gospel of connectedness. All refer to the dynamics of the triune interaction.

Meanwhile, our school classrooms continue to rank the cognition aspect of the learning process higher than the others, even though the body of research on the learning process does not elevate or place in competition against one another any single element of the tripartite

Perspectives on Cognition:

Philosophers:
*Reasoning; thinking*
Psychologists:
*Information processing; memory*
Cognitive Psychologists:
*Constructs of memory; understanding*
Learning Style Theorists:
*Neurological factors*
Brain-Based Learning Researchers:
*Neocortex-formal operations*

Perspectives on Conation:

Philosophers:
*Desire; behavior*
Psychologists:
*A determinant of behavior*
Cognitive Psychologists:
*Volition; self-regulated behavior*
Learning Style Theorists:
*Physicological factors*
Brain-Based Learning Researchers:
*Reptilian Complex; automatic behaviors*

A. G. Bell, cited in Gholar, Givens, McPherson, & Riggs, 1991

mind. Instead, the emphasis is on the interrelationship, interconnectedness, and holistic aspects of the mind.

## How Does Motivation Affect the Learning Process?

**Perspectives on Affectation:**

Philosophers:
*Feelings*
Psychologists:
*Feelings; values;*
*self-esteem*
Cognitive Psychologists:
*Self-efficacy; confidence*
Learning Style Theorists:
*Personality*
Brain-Based Learning
Researchers:
*Limbic system; emotions*

Dweck, 1986

Up to this point, we have reviewed a number of well-established components of the learning process but have not addressed the most troubling issue—motivation. What is it? How does it affect the learning process? The bottom line—what motivates the learner to learn? In our striving to put the learner at the center of the learning process, it is vital that we take the time to understand the relationship of motivation to learning and to understand what gives a person the internal drive to aspire to learn.

What motivates the learner to learn? Educational and cognitive psychologists have all types of answers. Their work identifies such elements of motivation as attention, interest, self-esteem, mindfulness, effort, and persistence. Some refer to motivation as a person-based trait, whereas others link motivation to the match between individual learning styles and the learning environment.

Most important, those studying the effects of interest and attention on the level of students' motivation concur that students do better with tasks that have relevance and challenge. Students are not motivated to master a "basic" skill by doing worksheets *ad nauseam;* they are motivated to do a task that focuses their abilities on a project that is relevant to their lives and challenges their abilities.

## Motivation in the Real World

**There is intrinsic motivation, and there is extrinsic motivation, and the greatest of these is intrinsic.**

Kahler, 1977

The proverb of motivation is as follows: There is intrinsic motivation, and there is extrinsic motivation, and the greatest of these is intrinsic.

The difficulty we as parents and teachers experience is that we can't get inside the student and punch the intrinsic "on" button or turn up its volume. Because we as teachers and parents can't modulate the internal, we seek to spur on the external. We do it with praise. We do it with criticism. We seek to motivate through the messages of "please me," "be perfect," "try hard," "be strong," and let's "hurry up" about it.

We also seek to motivate through rewards—the rewards of grades. Grades are more than just the representation of someone's achievement. We have reached the point at which teachers and students alike believe learning won't occur unless we have grades because grades spur the learner on to "try harder." Grades are used as a means of withholding approval, giving approval, or imposing disapproval—all as part of external motivation.

We also have systems today that have established other types of rewards. Recognition of achievement through certificates, scholarships, and credit cards at local fast-food establishments are means of externally motivating a child to learn. This type of motivation is based on an economy of "as long as you continue to pay me to do this, I will consider doing this." That type of remuneration as a means of motivating is purely calculating. Once the learner no longer needs or values the remuneration, the learner tunes out.

Extrinsic motivation is short-lived. Relying on it leaves the teacher always trying to second-guess what a student will respond to as an external reward. The student begins to think, "Oh, you want my interest? This is what you are going to have to do to keep my interest." "If my success as a student is based on your ability to externally motivate me, well then you'd better be on your toes coming up with interesting ideas that are going to turn me on in the classroom and keep me interested."

"Attention? I don't have a lot of attention. I've learned I don't need a long attention span. Things get resolved in nanoseconds on news broadcasts, in 30 minutes during sitcoms, and in 90 minutes minus commercials for docudramas. Wars are begun, lost, or won in less than 2 hours. So why would I invest myself in these learning games you are proposing? They are merely cheap gimmicks."

Students do see through this. They tire of sustaining interest in the learning process when they don't see any relevancy. Most students will go along with the entertainment value for awhile. I remember a history teacher who taught next door to my classroom. We used to call him Cecil B. DeMille. By the end of the first marking period, the students' interest in entering the world of history via video had worn off significantly. By the second marking period, the students referred to the class as a "time for snooze and news" (referring to the unauthorized taping and showing of the previous night's national news broadcasts).

If entertainment is the extrinsic motivation for learning and you lose the interest value, then you have lost the learner's interest, attention, and motivation. This becomes a taxing game played between the learner and the teacher. The teacher thinks, "I am doing my best. I am buying all these teacher aids and coming up with all these ideas and it still isn't doing the trick." *Trick* is probably the operative word here. We don't trick people into learning. What we do is give them the wherewithal to examine the learning process and allow them to develop their own commitment to using their will to learn.

The typical mistake we make in addressing motivation is to look for the quick fix. We look for a simple answer to motivation. Where is the place in the student's mind that we could feed chocolate ice cream and get a response? Where is the source of high-powered intrinsic motivation? This may not come as a big revelation to the reader, but it is necessary to say: There is *no* quick fix.

There is something much more powerful. It is called effort. Yes, effort. It is the same effort you first read about in Chapter 2 when I defined learning as a highly personal process by which we bring to bear our informed, engaged, and reflective effort to develop our ability to know, to do, and to feel. It is the totality of who we are interacting with

**Perspectives on Motivation:**

Philosophers:
  *The spark that moves the heart and mind*
Psychologists:
  *A focused effort to accomplish a task linked to self-esteem, self-efficacy*
Cognitive Psychologists:
  *A predecisional state; the concept of self-regulation linked to interest, attention, and persistence*
Learning Style Theorists:
  *The outcome of matching student learning style to classroom instruction style; teacher teaching style*
Brain-Based Learning Researchers:
  *The engagement of self*

**We don't trick people into learning.**

Barrett, 1931

our mental processes. *Effort is intrinsically situated and externally displayed.* It is this effort that motivates us—moves us—to learn.

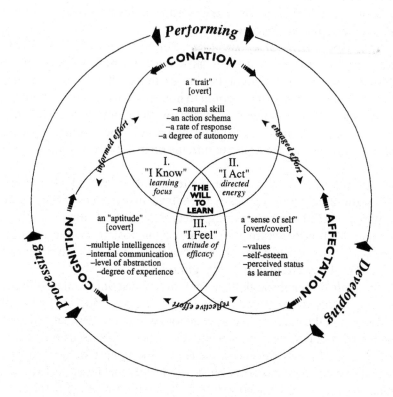

**Figure 4.2.** The Interactive Learning Model

# 5

The will is the integrating force of the individual.
—Assagioli, 1973, p. 9

# Where There Is a Will, There Is a Learner

## The Will at Last

You, as a reader, are by now starting to realize how this book got its title. The answer will soon appear. Even now, you may begin to notice that a faint drumroll is rapidly building to a crescendo. At last, the message that drives this text: The will to learn is the very heart of the learning process.

The will is a specific power which rises up within each of us to give the individual the inner energy to wrestle, cope with, and integrate the whole of ourself.
—Assagioli, 1973, p. 9

**The will to learn is the very heart of the learning process.**

## The Will at First

For centuries, the will has been closely aligned with the concept of motivation. It has been described as the passion, the energy, the drive-within motivation that moves individuals to action. Modern day psychologists refer to *will* as the drive to act that is uniquely our own. *Will* is that force that is derived from our sense of deep meaning—our sense of purpose—our drive to have meaning. Meaning arouses our energy. The energy of meaning is our passion. The energy to act on what is meaningful forms the very heart of our will.

What would happen if the students' learning process took center stage in our classrooms? What would happen if we could help students unlock their passion to learn? What would happen if, instead of coaching, prodding, and even bribing our students for their attention,

Deep Meaning
↓
Energy
↓
Passion
↓
The Will
—Caine & Caine, 1991

de Chardin, 1923/1959

Jung, 1923

Snow & Jackson, 1992

Elliot, 1986

| **The Will** | |
|---|---|
| Philosophers | Intelligent energy directed toward a definite aim |
| Psychologists | The sum of psychic energy |
| Cognitive psychologists | Likened to drive, volition—it is part of the conative constructs |
| Learning style theorists | [not mentioned in the literature] |
| Brain-based learning researchers | The governor of the left and right hemispheres |

Box 5.1.

we helped them engage their wills for the purpose of learning? What would happen if we listened to the students—if we sought to work collaboratively with them to unlock their will to learn?

To truly understand the will, we need to go back to some statements made in earlier chapters. We need to revisit the Child's Learning Adventure (Chapter 2). We need to add another key word. The word is *why*. In the earliest stages of schooling, the child has little opportunity to ask, "Why?" No, not the why of "Why does this happen or how does this occur?" Here I am referring to the bigger *why:* the why of "Why is this (activity) important to do? Why do I need to know this? Why am I sitting here learning in this manner? Why don't I feel better about what I am asked to do?" This is the *why* of meaning. It seeks to find purpose, meaning, and relevance.

The why question does not appear on the Child's Learning Adventure chart because during the first years, the child is uncomfortable challenging what appears to be a well-run machine. Although outwardly the child is conforming to the school day, the school curriculum, and the schoolteacher, inwardly the child is questioning the relevance of what she or he is asked to do.

Eventually, **Why?** looms in bold letters before the learner. **Why** the mindless learning represented by rote memorization, fill in the _____, 50-50 games of chance (otherwise known as true-and-false), and in-my-memory-today-gone-tomorrow? The more I am asked to perform in this way, the less enthusiastic I am about being here. These activities only reinforce my bewilderment. **Why** this activity? **Why** this assignment? **Why** test me like this?

The relevance of the why question becomes clearer in the oft-repeated responses of more than 4,500 children living within and outside of the United States to the question, "If I were the teacher, how would I teach?" "I would have us learn things that I can use in everyday life." "I would make learning relevant." "I would have my students learn things away from school." "I would go and see how to do things

Any teacher who hasn't heard the big *Why?* at least a dozen times a day from students, and very possibly colleagues as well, simply isn't listening carefully.

The system of schooling, unsure of how to respond to the boldness and/or insolence, reacts with, "Just do it, and Please Me and Hurry Up about it."
—D. Hallworth, written

Johnston, 1996

in the real world." Relevance, relevance, relevance. Application, application, application. Meaning, meaning, meaning.

Learners want the time and opportunity to see how these disparate parts of schooling—reading, math, science, social studies, English, and on and on—fit together. They want to be able to discover the wholeness of learning. This is what will spark their will to learn. This is what unlocks their will and engages their motivation to process, perform, and develop as learners. Anything less is meaningless.

The will to learn is the degree to which the learner is prepared to invest in the learning process. What a difference an understanding of will could make for learners! What a difference an understanding of will could make for us as teachers!

The current development of integrated curricula is a significant attempt to address the why question.

**The will to learn is the degree to which the learner is prepared to invest in the learning process.**

# 6

If there is to be a common theoretical base for the concept of learning style, it will be found in an integrated model of person-situation interaction and adaptation.
—Snow & Jackson, 1992, pp. 84-85

# Putting It All Together

## Regurgitation or Revelations

As you will recall, three chapters ago I set out to explore the literature and research that explains the process of learning. Following is the outcome of that inquiry. I have chosen to represent that outcome in the form of the Interactive Learning Model. Its configuration and its explanation are forged from the learning of others. It is a synthesis of what we know. It has come from stirring, mixing, and reflecting on the work of others. It has a philosophical basis, an empirical basis, and a reflective basis. It is not based on a new revelation; it is based on insights from an examination of what others have perceived as to how we learn. It moves the body of knowledge about the learning process a smidgen forward.

*Smidgen* here is defined as a humble awareness that much is yet to be understood about the complexity of the learning process.

## The Learner at the Center of the Learning Process

Snow and Jackson (1992) comment on this lack of a conceptualization in their catalog of conative constructs.

During this "dig" into the literature, nowhere did I find a depiction of the learner's cognition, conation, and affectation as an interactive process even though the literature emphasizes the triune nature of these mental faculties. In response to the need for a model representing such interaction, I have developed the Interactive Learning Model.

To describe the learning process, I chose the metaphor of a combination lock. I conceptualize cognition, conation, and affectation as interlocking tumblers that when aligned, unlock an individual's understanding of his or her learning combination. I metaphorically picture the intricate interaction of cognition (processing), conation (performing), and affectation (developing) as the numerals of the lock's combination. Each individual's learning combination, thus, is composed of cognitive-conative-affective interaction.

The learner may initiate the learning process by reviewing his or her bank of prior learning for clues on how to make sense of the current task. Throughout the cognitive processing, the learner seeks to identify what aptitude or intelligence is needed to "crack" the learning task. While identifying and initiating cognitive processing, the learner simultaneously instigates the performance of the task.

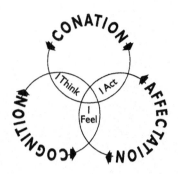

The "doing" process reflects the learner's conative performing trait. Conative performance consists of an individual's natural talent to perform (skill), rate of response (pace), and desire to work alone or in groups (autonomy). This interaction leads to another turn of the lock's dial, which produces the learner's affective development. Here the interaction continues with the learner's sense of status as a learner triggering a complementary level of self-esteem and producing an outlook of confidence and a willingness to persist in engaging in similar tasks in the future.

## The Interactive Learning Model

Interaction is the key. It is the operative term for this model. The interaction depicted here occurs among the three faculties of the mind. The interaction contributes to the wholeness of the learner's response. The nature of the interaction builds the basis of the learner's motivation.

## Motivation—Interactive Style

As the learner sifts through the incoming stimuli and organizes, labels, grasps, or plays with them, the learner uses *informed effort.* Simultaneously, *engaged effort* moves into action as the learner applies interest, attention, and self-regulation to performing the mental or physical task ahead. It is this engagement of effort that heightens the learner's level of motivation, simultaneously causing the learner to stand back and reflect on his or her development of knowledge and skill. This use of *reflective effort* continues to feed the entire learning process.

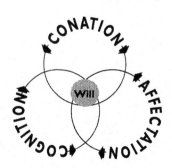

## The Will—Interactive Style

The will lies at the center of this model. It is the place where things come together for an individual, where there is that sense of knowing

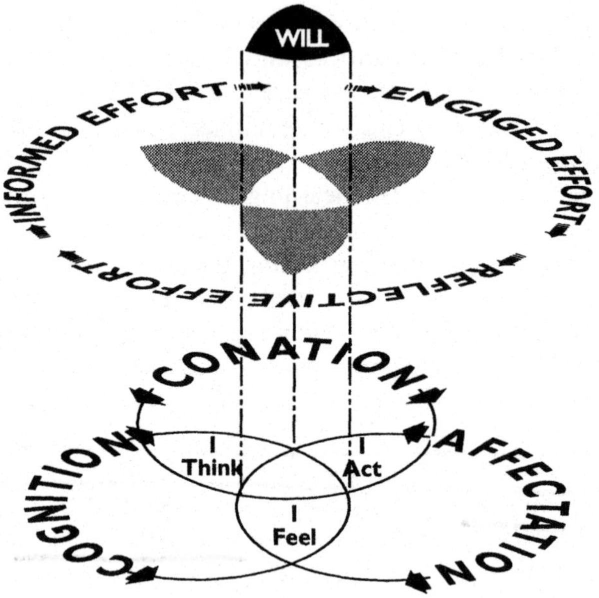

**Figure 6.1.** Dimensions of the Interactive Learning Model
SOURCE: Johnston (1995). Copyright © 1995 by C. Johnston. Used by permission.

about oneself, an understanding that one is going to be able to learn, to do the learning task, and to take the challenge and succeed.

## Unlocking the Lock

We can put this complex process in a much simpler context. We begin with a student standing in front of her locker. She rotates the dial, completes the combination, and opens the locker in which she has stored books, materials, and personal items, all for use while in school. As she begins the process, she asks herself, "Uh, what did I stop by to pick up?" The student's *informed effort* begins. "Oh, yeah, I know. But what is it I need to complete the assignment? Let's see; we're doing that role play. I need my props for that." The learner's *engaged effort* for learning mounts. "This ought to be a neat experience. I like doing this kind of learning. I get a kick out of ad-libbing." *Reflective effort* has assisted the student in completing the final turn of the dial. The lock yields. The plane of involvement has shifted to a higher level—the level of the will. The locker is open. Here the self-actualized, energized, totally engaged individual is submersed in preparation for learning: all three aspects of the brain firing, all three mental faculties operating to capacity, all three divisions of the mind engaged.

The will to learn prepares us to invest ourselves in the learning process.

**The will to learn prepares us to invest ourselves in the learning process.**

# Chapter

## 7

Education is not something we do to people. Education is something people do for themselves—assisted we hope by the efforts of teachers.
—Fenstermacher, 1990, as paraphrased in Levin, 1994, p. 759

# Making Our Lists and Checking Them Twice

## List 1: The Learner's List

As teachers preparing to enter the 21st century, we need to reaffirm for the learner, the learner's parents, and our schools who is to be center stage in education.

### It is the learner.

We need to remember what encompasses the process of learning.

### It is the whole person.

We need to focus on the central issue of education.

### It is the learner and the learning process.

We need to invest ourselves as learners and teachers of learners in respecting and contributing to each other's learning process. And finally, we need to challenge the schooling process to accept the learner and to create an environment in which the learner can thrive. Although

---

**Learner's List**

✓ Energized

✓ Reflective

✓ Responsible

✓ Valued

✓ Respected

the learner's list is vital to developing a healthy sense of what school is to be about, the teacher's list serves an equally important role. The teacher's list declares our mission.

## List 2: The Teacher's List

Our vision of a learning environment in which the student is fully valued and considered in all phases of educational planning leads us as teachers to formulate a mission statement to serve as our guide into the next century.

---

**Our mission as teachers of learners of the 21st century is to**

- Engage, nurture, and respect the whole learner
- Provide knowledge and skills to enable the retrieval and use of effective communication of information
- Provide opportunities for autonomous problem solving
- Provide weekly occasions to explore and experiment within and beyond the physical boundaries of the classroom

---

**Box 7.1.**

*Unlocking the Will to Learn* speaks to this mission. It examines the learner-student from both the learner-student's and teacher-learner's perspectives. Its purpose is to help both become better learners as they develop the skill and will to learn.

The underlying premise behind *Unlocking the Will to Learn* is that learners learn best when given the opportunity to understand their learning process.

## List 3: The Learning Model List

| Learning Model List |
| :--- |
| ✓ Understandable |
| ✓ Authentic |
| ✓ Applicable |

The Interactive Learning Model, the basis for the discussion that follows in Parts 2 and 3, provides an authentic model of the learning process—one that represents the learner's motivation and will to learn—without putting an additional burden on the teacher. It begins by looking at the wholeness, rather than the parts and pieces, of the learner. The model helps the learner be prepared to engage in the learning process as an energized and reflective learner who understands his or her responsibility for the learning. At the same time, the Interactive Learning Model helps the teacher respect and value the learner. Above all, the Interactive Learning Model returns the learner to the learner's rightful place—center stage in the process of learning.

# PART

# 2

# FINDING THE PATTERNS

## Before We Continue

Part 1 examined who the learner is, how the learner learns, and what the central issues of learning are. We established the importance of having the learner be center stage, and we established the Interactive Learning Model as a realistic representation of how learning occurs. At some point in the text, I hope you caught yourself shaking your head in agreement as a result of having found yourself among the descriptions of the student, the learner, and the teacher.

In Part 2, the learner is viewed within the context of patterns of learning behaviors or schemas. The voice, actions, and feelings that accompany each pattern are carefully examined. The interaction of these patterns is also studied. You can plan on seeing yourself once again in these pages as your awareness of yourself as an interactive learner grows.

# Chapter

**8**

Life all around me here in the
village:
Tragedy, comedy, valor and
truth,
All in the loom, and oh what
patterns!
Blind to all of it all my life long.
—Masters, *Spoon River Anthology*,
1915/1992, p. 173

# Looking for the Whole With an Eye for Pattern

## Looking Where the Action Is

Last evening, you spent hours preparing for today's class. You studied your "palette" of multiple intelligences and chose to use at least five options for student learning activities. You even wrote down the directions to make certain they would be clear. You were sure this would be a good lesson.

Gardner, 1983

Now here you are today, 2 minutes into the activity, and Dale has his hand up asking a question about the exact number of words you expect for each paragraph. He chose Option I, "Building a Fact Pyramid," but as usual your directions weren't specific enough for him. He wants to know exactly what it is you expect. He also wants to know how many sources you want him to use. He says he read an article in the local newspaper about this. Can he use that information?

Gary, your "quiet one," seemed to listen to the directions, but now he is sitting with his notebook closed staring out the window totally disengaged. Try as you might, you never seem to come up with an option that grabs his interest. It is so frustrating. He isn't a bad kid. He's pleasant, but he really isn't a good student.

Chris never waited for you to finish the explanation of the assignment before she started, and already you can tell she's not following the directions. Lord, give me strength! She hears more than a different drummer; she has her own band playing tunes inside her. You probably couldn't come up with an activity that suited her just because it wasn't her own idea!

And then there's Mardi. Thank heavens for Mardi. She always follows directions. In fact, she keeps you on your toes when it comes to giving directions. If the directions aren't clear enough, she will let you know. There she is, on task, carefully working her way through Option II and checking off each step as she completes the assignment. (It appears she is going to do a musical project.) It's now 5 minutes into the assignment, and she is the only student on task.

How is this possible? What went wrong? You followed the multiple intelligences (MI) literature; you were sensitive to the learning styles of these students. After all, they have plenty of options by which to show their work. What happened to this well-planned lesson? How could this be happening again to you, a conscientious teacher?

The answer is, "Nothing went wrong." The teacher trap that you have fallen into is a common one. It's the trap of "I teach, students learn. I teach multiple intelligences; students will learn using at least one of them. I teach to their style; students will learn using their style." But we learned in Part 1 that the responsibility for learning is the student's and that it is the student who is center stage in this process, not the teacher.

We also identified the complexity of the interactive learning process—the nonlinearity of it. We agreed that teachers create a learning environment in which the interactive process of learning occurs. We learned that it is very much an individual process, a self-regulated process, an interactive process. Now, if after reading the opening scenario, you have come to the conclusion that just reading about the process wasn't enough, you are correct. There is more to understanding the interactive learning process.

Gardner, 1989

## Looking at the Patterns

The first thing to recognize is that the interactive process does not occur on a random basis. It occurs as a pattern of behaviors. These behaviors are formed from the combination of our cognitive, conative, and affective tendencies. These tendencies converge to form the basis of our thought processes, mode of action, and feelings about ourselves. This convergence also forms our patterns of learning behavior.

Notice I emphasize the word *patterns* because as you will soon read, there is good reason to believe that our learning process consists of a mixture of at least four patterns: one sequential, one precise, one technical, and one confluent.

## Patterns All Around Us

Each summer, when I was between the ages of 8 and 13, I spent 2 weeks with a friend of my mother in Milwaukee, Wisconsin. She was

the "Mrs. Wizard" of my life. Anita had so many talents and skills—she could craft jewelry in her workshop, develop photographs in her downstairs laboratory, do intricate rosemaling, and construct the most fascinating array of delicate paper mobiles. Her greatest talent lay in her ability to weave. At night I would fall asleep listening to the back-and-forth swish of the shuttle and thump-clump as she shifted the peddles of her room-sized loom. Thread by thread, the skeletal warp became a patterned fabric. It is from this experience that I have come to appreciate the structuring of patterns.

Our human systems are fashioned in much the same way. We, too, consist of intricate patterns of behavior. The patterns within us have parallels to the tangible fabrics that clothe our lives—the plaids, ginghams, and so forth. A plaid, for example, is formed by perpendicular lines carefully designed to provide an overall effect of structure and consistency, whereas the pattern of gingham is based on precision. The check of the gingham may vary in size, but not in exactness. Unlike gingham or plaid, jacquard does not follow a prescribed formula. It is formed solely by the hand of the weaver. The pattern may be as simple as an occasional thread of muted color or as subtle as a tiny fleck, a fine distinction in the otherwise staid woof of the fabric. Designer paisley, the most random of patterns, also exhibits the greatest visual flow. To look closely at a paisley is to gain one perspective; to see a paisley at a distance is to gain another.

In a similar fashion, our learning behaviors consist of characteristics woven together. In this case, the threads of cognition, conation, and affectation form learning patterns. The cognitive strands of intellectual ability (mental acuity, memory, range of experiences, and level of abstractions or concreteness), the conative cords of natural skill (pace, autonomy, and engaged energy) and the affective threads of feelings (values and sense of self) form a range of learning patterns from ancestral plaid, to meticulous gingham, to highly crafted jacquard, to outrageous paisley.

## Not a Plot, a Pattern: Scheme, Schema, Schemas

For some of you, the metaphor of fabric may be too artsy, too ethereal—you want the real stuff of science. Patterns, smatterns! How do we know that these aren't just the whimsy of some inventive mind? The answer to that is found in science. Much of science talks about patterns. Even chaos theory refers to "forms in motion," "patterns born amid formlessness." Those who espouse this view of science also point to the brain as an example of "dynamic systems." These individuals charge that "cognitive scientists can no longer model the mind as a static structure." No argument there!

Gleick, 1987, pp. 5, 299

Cognitive scientists from the United Kingdom, Europe, and the United States who have studied human behavior have long held that the mind operates through the use of patterning. Their term for these patterns is *schema*. A schema is a mental configuration of experience

*Webster's,* 1991

Ach, 1935
Atkinson & Birch, 1970
Sander, 1930, p. 202

Pay, 1981, p. 4
Kolb, 1984, p. 97

Keefe & Languis, 1983, as
quoted in Keefe & Ferrell, 1990,
p. 59

**Perspectives on Schemas:**

Philosophers:
*The productive
imagination through
which the
understanding is able
to apply its categories
to experience*
Neuropsychology:
*The automatic
unconscious
organization of
incoming
physiological or
psychological stimuli*
Cognitive Psychologists:
*Structures that have
references to our
categories of action
sequences*

Philip, 1936, pp. 30-38

that includes a particular organized way of perceiving cognitively and responding to a complex situation or set of stimuli. The schemas form the framework in which the learner operates.

Their work on the patterns of learning behaviors suggests that we each have distinct schemas or patterns of behavior. One researcher described schemas as "structural tendencies pressing again and again for a satisfactory conclusion; chaos falling into visible order; fragmentary items acquiring meaning and long sought and suspected connections suddenly flashing into mind." Others refer to these schemas as "patterns of activation and organization," "individual possibility-processing structures," or "consistent patterns of transactions with the world." Cognitive science describes the schema as the composite characteristics of cognitive, affective, and physiological factors that serve as "relatively stable indicators of how a learner perceives, interacts with and responds to the environment."

Up to this point, I have chosen not to sprinkle the text with academic references. Instead, I've placed notes in the margin for those who want to do further reading on the research that forms the basis of this book. I am now going to deviate from that practice, however, and digress to relate a study reported in 1936 by Howard Philip.

Briefly, Philip, a cognitive psychologist, recruited participants to be observed while solving nonmathematical "puzzles" or what today we call "mind-benders." The number of puzzles solved by each participant under clinically orchestrated and timed circumstances totaled more than 300!

As the participants worked to solve each puzzle, they were carefully observed. Their heart and pulse rates were taken, their physical behaviors were observed, and their spoken comments were meticulously recorded. At the completion of each day's work, the participants were individually interviewed about the thoughts and feelings they experienced as they engaged in each task. Philip then cataloged his subjects' reflections, placing them into three categories: cognitive, conative, and affective. Of special interest to us is his recording of key words and phrases used by the participants as they described their problem-solving experiences.

I was determined to solve it *in order.*

I concentrated on *grasping the details. . . .* My volition did not take place until *I grasped the details.*

Once again *I had to check my desire to begin before the directions were read* and understood.

I made a conscious effort *to wrestle with the problem as a whole.*

*With very few seconds' concentration,* I found the solution; *I didn't need to verify* the solution before I signalled back.

My method was very easy. *I ran through as many names as I could remember.*

My method was "trial and error."

I *began with my usual method* of trying to get combinations.

I'm not certain that is a word, but *I'll risk it.*

The *whole question struck me on the first reading as meaningless, and I gave up* and waited for the buzzer.

I *exactly retraced the steps* which led to the obstruction.

I *commenced in a methodical way.*

I think the chief feeling all the time was that *I was in a hurry.* The hurry accounts for the *wild guesses.*

This study and others have found similar categories of responses—suggesting that there is a consistency to our behavioral schemas. These patterns of natural tendencies become of key interest to us as we seek to understand the patterns of our interactive learning and as we seek to unlock our will to learn.

There is a set of recognizable phenomenon which roughly speaking involve the will. What they have in common is relevance to situations—to initiating and carrying on actions and getting things done.
—M. Warnock, cited in Pears, 1963, p. 15

## Schemas in Learners' Terms

Just like a behavioral schema, a learning schema is a pattern of behaviors that has formed through time. It comes from our "natural tendencies" of behavior. Interactively, these patterns immerse the learner in processing, performing, and reflecting on the basis of sequence and organization, specificity and precision, technical performance and reasoning, and confluence and intuition. Each is distinct from the other; each contributes to the other; each builds the wholeness of our learning process.

When we seek to unlock the will to learn, we are seeking to have learners unlock the knowledge of what these schemas are. We are seeking to have learners understand how the patterns interact. We are seeking to have them know which pattern they naturally choose to use first and which to use last—even to avoid if possible.

We want each learner to have an awareness of "Uh, I know why I am feeling what I'm feeling. I know why I'm approaching this the way I am. It's okay. My patterns and schemas are not weird or wrong—they are what I bring to learning."

## My Four Schemas: Up Close and Personal

The sequential pattern is that part of me that seeks order and consistency. "I process information step by step. I act according to the rules. I want time to present a neat and complete assignment. I may need time to double-check what I have done. Don't rush me, please."

Another part of my overall pattern wants to know exactly what is going on. "I process information precisely. I read it precisely; I write it precisely; I store it precisely; and I respond to it precisely. I feel good

The order in which the schemas are presented here and in ensuing chapters is for ease of the reader and in no way suggests a ranking of the patterns.

about myself as a student when I get precise feedback and when I am able to point to specific things I've done that have earned me recognition."

A part of my learning pattern processes technically, using stand-alone, independent reasoning. That part of me says, "Let me figure this out; let me do this by myself. This is where I use my technical know-how. I see an instrument or a tool, and I know its use. More than that, I am intrigued and fascinated by its form and function—I know how it operates. I especially like the physical and mental challenge of using it successfully to do whatever the situation requires."

There is also a confluent part to my learning pattern. It pulls together all the areas of my experience—my knowledge—even my nickel knowledge—and forms them into a sense of "I've been here before. I understand this territory. This is how this fits together." It's the confluence of what I take with me into each task that I do. It is also that part of me that says, "Okay. So you haven't been here before. So what. Make a guess. Take the risk." This part of me works on intuition rather than specific information or structure or knowledge of how something works. I go with my gut. I have a sense—not a measurable sense—but an intuitive sense of how to proceed, and I move on that. I don't mind failing. I can always start again with a new idea." This part of me takes pleasure in the totality of who I am—all I can bring to bear on the situation from my various experiences.

## A Cast of Characters

When we look at our original scenario and place each student within the patterns described above, we see each learner differently. For instance, Dale isn't preparing to be a game show host. His questions are sincere, and, for him, answers to these questions are important. He wants to know information because he enjoys knowing things for the sake of knowing them.

Gary isn't avoiding the assignment because he resents you. He has now been inside classrooms for the better part of 4 hours. He needs space, and he needs to see the relevance of sitting for another 45 minutes doing this assignment. He thinks he could do this better if he were away from this environment. He needs to know why he is feeling what he is feeling even as his classmates dig into an assignment that doesn't make any sense to him.

Chris isn't being rude or difficult when she doesn't wait until all the directions are given. Her head is ready to burst with different ways to do this assignment and she can't wait to begin. She isn't worried about doing the assignment incorrectly. She is concerned about making her work uniquely her own. No need for directions if you aren't tied to doing the assignment in only one way.

And Mardi hasn't "behaved" in the manner described earlier because she has an interest in music. She has gone about doing the assignment by carefully following the teacher's directions because Mardi likes structure. She is going to follow directions and apply strong

The craftsman applies values, technical reasoning, and all of his faculties to performing a given task in a non-fragmented manner.
—Tempte, 1991, p. 163

organization to whatever she does because that is her dominant learning pattern. She may employ a great deal of neatness in whatever she does, and she even may want time to double-check her work. It isn't her musical ability that has framed her response to the assignment; it is her pattern of interactive learning that has formed her response.

## Pattern Alert—Pattern Awareness

We don't know all there is to know about these learners from just observing them in the classroom, but we do know each has a distinct pattern. Dale wants precise information; Gary seeks a different type of learning challenge than the paper-and-pencil options offered; Chris wants to do her own thing; Mardi wants to get the project done according to Hoyle.

Not immediately clear from these classroom observations is the complexity of the mix composing each learner. All four schemas are present in each of us in greater and lesser degrees. The following chapter provides a more in-depth description of each of the schemas that make up the Interactive Learning Model. The chapter examines each using vivid examples and the voices of the learners. They say it better than my words ever could.

9

Behind the particular visible shapes of matter are ghostly forms serving as invisible templates.
—Plato, cited in Thompson, 1961, p. 8

# Doubting Thomases Need Not Apply, or Seeing Is Believing

## Schema 101: Slide Presentation

I am now going to use a series of "slides." I admit this is a novel approach; I can think of no better vehicle, however, for demonstrating the work-product of the four schemas. For this purpose, I have chosen to use student exams. I have selected four different responses—each representing a different learning schema. I am going to ask you to follow along as we examine each slide, looking for visual evidence of the characteristics described in your reading up to this point.

### *Slide One*

Here we have the typical response of the individual whose primary schema is sequential processing. In this case, the individual drew a chart in lieu of writing out her answer in a narrative form. Note the use of hand-drawn lines to establish demarcation between the historic periods.

Furthermore, note the use of dashes before the items and the use of asterisks to identify important periods of history. Observe the neatness and consistency of the response.

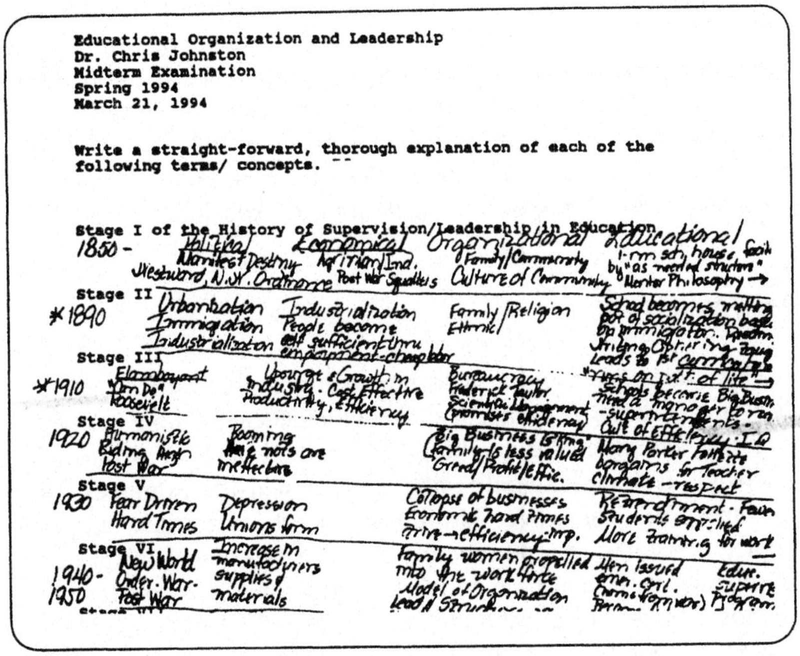
Educational Organization and Leadership
Dr. Chris Johnston
Midterm Examination
Spring 1994
March 21, 1994

Write a straight-forward, thorough explanation of each of the following terms/ concepts.

Stage I of the History of Supervision/Leadership in Education
1850 - Political Economical Organizational Educational

Stage II
*1890

Stage III
*1910

Stage IV
1920

Stage V
1930

Stage VI
1940- 1950

**Figure 9.1.**

## *Slide Two*

Slide Two depicts the major performance behaviors of an individual whose primary schema is precise processing. Several characteristics are

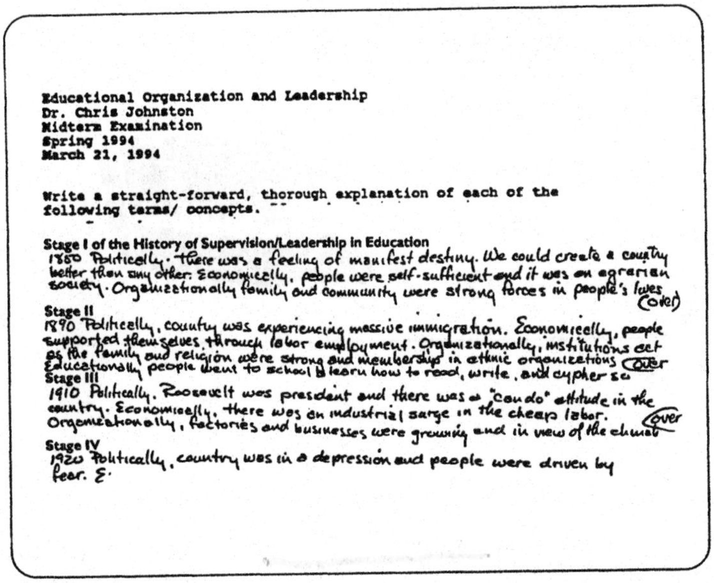
Educational Organization and Leadership
Dr. Chris Johnston
Midterm Examination
Spring 1994
March 21, 1994

Write a straight-forward, thorough explanation of each of the following terms/ concepts.

Stage I of the History of Supervision/Leadership in Education
1850 Politically - there was a feeling of manifest destiny. We could create a country better than any other. Economically, people were self-sufficient and it was an agrarian society. Organizationally family and community were strong forces in people's lives (over)

Stage II
1890 Politically, country was experiencing massive immigration. Economically, people supported themselves through labor employment. Organizationally, institutions act as the family and religion were strong and membership in ethnic organizations (over) Educationally people went to school to learn how to read, write, and cypher so

Stage III
1910 Politically. Roosevelt was president and there was a "can do" attitude in the country. Economically, there was an industrial surge in the cheap labor. Organizationally, factories and businesses were growing and in view of the climate (over)

Stage IV
1920 Politically, country was in a depression and people were driven by fear. E.

**Figure 9.2.**

of note. First, examine the detail that this student used in answering each response. As a part of the detail, note the number of words. Take special consideration of the word that lies circled at what you would expect to be the end of the answer. The circled word is *over.* The student has continued each answer on the reverse side of the page. The back side of the page is as filled with data and information as is the front. Note also that these answers are written in an expository style.

### Slide Three

This slide represents a most interesting example of a technical processing schema. The student spoke with the teacher long before the exam date and asked for an alternative method of demonstrating his knowledge. He said he would rather capture real-life examples using videotapes. His voice-over introduction to the materials, although complete, is stated in a perfunctory manner. His actual script of the miniproduction is short on written content and long on technical directions. He said he left it up to the people to do the talking. He was just there to capture their actions. The videos themselves show skill in both filming and editing—a skill the classroom teacher said she was unaware the student possessed.

**Figure 9.3.**

### Slide Four

This slide represents confluent processing. It might best be labeled "Hit and Run." The student has "hit" the high points of information, believing the teacher should be able to fill in from there. Note the use

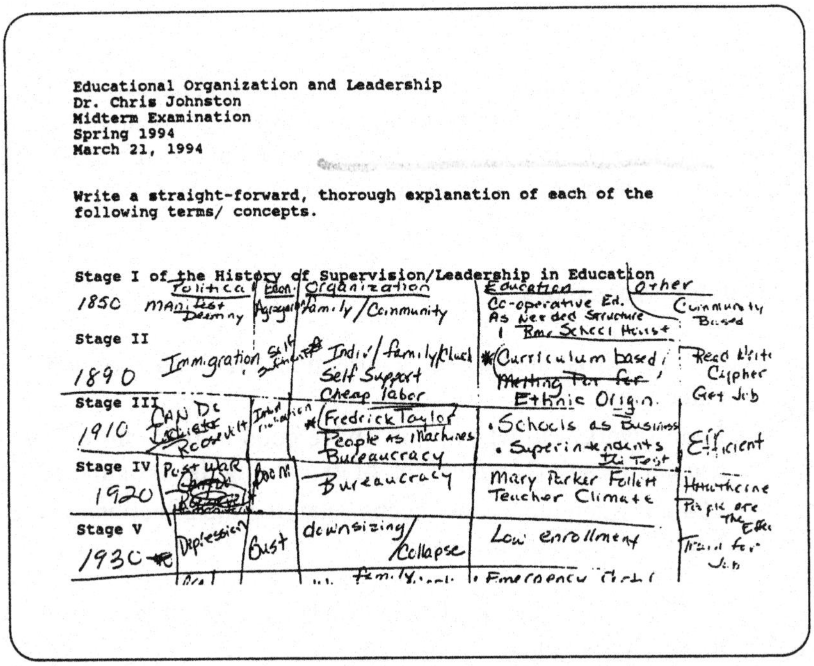

Educational Organization and Leadership
Dr. Chris Johnston
Midterm Examination
Spring 1994
March 21, 1994

Write a straight-forward, thorough explanation of each of the
following terms/ concepts.

Stage I of the History of Supervision/Leadership in Education

*[handwritten chart on examination showing Stages I–V with dates 1850, 1890, 1910, 1920, 1930 and columns Political, Econ., Organization, Education, Other]*

**Figure 9.4.**

*[handwritten margin note:]*

Schema —
Mental configuration of
experiences that includes
a particular organized
way of perceiving & responding
to a complex situation

schemas
―――――――
1 sequential
Processing

2 precise
Processing

3 Technical
Processing

4 Confluent
Processing

of abbreviations, symbols, and catchy phrases. Observe the slanted writing placed at different angles. I see this as an attempt to make the answers fit into the hastily drawn boxes. Do you see the cross-outs? The unevenness of the charted lines?

This slide indicates that the student was not concerned about neatness or completeness. This student was interested in getting the test over with and moving on to another activity.

## Schema 102: Out of the Mouths of Learners

Well, if seeing isn't believing, maybe "hearing" is. I have filled the following paragraphs—no, I have *packed* the following paragraphs— with example after example of the voices of student learners and their responses to three simple questions:

- What makes learning frustrating for you?
- How would you teach students to learn?
- How would you like to show the teacher what you know?

On the following pages are the answers to those questions—not answers given by 10 or 20 or even 1,000 students but answers given by more than 4,500 students 6 to 22 years of age located within the United States and abroad.

Just as the Schema 101: Slide Presentation identified common characteristics of each learning schema, Schema 102: Out of the Mouths of Learners reports the common expressions found in students' responses. The responses themselves describe the interactive schema that drives their

Part 3 reports the means by which these responses were gathered.

will to learn. No editing, no descriptive state, just plain words written or spoken so frequently that they have earned the distinction of being called "standard representative responses." I have categorized the comments for the purpose of emphasis and ease of the reader.

## Sequential Processors

The Seeker of Clear Directions

- I become frustrated when the directions aren't clear or don't make sense.
- I don't work well when I don't have good instructions or the teacher doesn't do a good job of explaining the assignment.
- I hate it when the teacher keeps changing the directions in the middle of the assignment.

The Practiced Planner

- It's hard when the teacher isn't organized or doesn't explain things thoroughly.
- I want the teacher to go over and over the assignment until I understand it.
- I like the teacher to go slow and make sure everybody is at the same spot.
- I always practice my answers by going over and over them.
- I like plenty of in-class practice.

The Thoroughly Neat Worker

- I need time to study and to complete the work in class.
- I'm frustrated when the teacher gives us lots of worksheets and no time to do the work and go over it in class.
- I don't like it when I don't have enough time to do a thorough job.
- I need time to make my work look neat and to make sure my answers are correct.
- I don't want my work to look sloppy so I need time to do the work neatly.

## Precise Processors

The Information Specialist

- I want to know all the answers; I want to know what will be on the test.
- I like the teacher to see that my work is correct.
- I'm frustrated when I don't know all the answers because I like doing the work right so that I get a good grade.
- I am frustrated when I don't have enough information or I can't find the information and the answers aren't in the book.

– I become frustrated when the teacher doesn't go into detail and explain things. Confusion!

– I would have students take notes and do activities to reinforce the information.

– I like trivia. I'm good at that.

– I take detailed notes and then go over and over them.

The Into-Details Researcher

– I like to show people what I know by answering all of the teacher's questions.

– I like to take tests and quizzes to show what I know.

– If you want to know what I know, read my answers or ask me questions.

The Answer Specialist

– I have a better voice when I am writing than when speaking publicly.

– I need time and length to prove what I am saying when I am writing.

– I like to show what I know by writing a several page paper and looking stuff up.

The Report Writer

## Technical Processors √

– I want hands-on activities which interest me instead of taking notes, doing book work, or writing about it.

– Give me the tools and let me demonstrate what I know hands-on.

– Let me build things!

– Give me a real challenging project with a point to it and let me figure it out.

The Hands-On Builder

– I need to run around outside and get things to make sense in my head.

– Let students have more breaks during the day to go outside.

– Let me learn by going home and living and experiencing it.

– Let students learn however they want.

– I don't let the teacher know what I know.

– I am a very private person. I keep it inside.

– I don't want to show a teacher what I know. I'm happy the way I am.

– Let me work at home where there is no one to bother me.

The Independent Private Thinker

– I learn better from real-world experiences.

– I learn by living what I learn.

– Take me out into the real world and show me something.

The Reality Seeker

### Confluent Processors

— I am frustrated when I feel trapped in the teacher's ideas. That's when I don't even feel like doing the assignment.

— I'm frustrated when I come up with a certain idea and I'm not allowed to do it.

**The Different Drummer**

— I don't like having to do an assignment in one certain way.

— I don't like having to do the same things as everybody else.

— I don't like following lots of rules and regulations.

— I like to use my imagination.

— I like exploring new things.

**The Creative Imaginer**

— I like to work with people who are curious and don't do assignments in just one way.

— I like learning in a creative, fun, entertaining way.

— I like coming up with artistic and crafty things.

— I like to do storytelling where you use pictures and your own imagination.

— I like to write things the same way I'd say them.

— I like writing stories using my own ideas and not some dumb book.

**The Unique Presenter**

— I like to do skits and dress-up like historic persons.

— I like to stand up and talk.

— I like to express myself through oral presentations, skits, and creative projects.

## Could P. D. James Be Wrong?

I began this chapter by presenting the visual, auditory, and student-authored examples of four distinct learning schemas. I think presenting the information in this manner most clearly verifies the existence of—and student use of—the four learning schemas. Now I think it is time to look at each schema more closely. I do this by building a learner profile—yes, a type of identikit—so that the reader can begin to recognize the nature of learner behaviors in the classroom. The descriptions that follow don't require visual aids. We who teach are able to see each of them clearly in our mind's eye.

Before I begin the following in-depth look at each learning pattern, I want to make a disclaimer. I don't want the focused nature of the information that follows to detract from the central point of this text—that the learner is a person, a whole person. Not a left brain; not a right brain. Not two intelligences or five. Not SAT scores. Not state proficiencies. Not one schema; not one learning pattern.

A classification is most useful if it helps one to recognize and understand different types that already exist within the scheme of nature.
—Allport, 1961, p. 356

The learner is a whole person. That wholeness consists of patterns of cognition, conation, and affectation. That wholeness consists of the physical, mental, and spiritual qualities—of a whole human being—in a real world setting.

The identikits that follow do not look at the whole learner. For the purpose of emphasis and clarity, each focuses on one of the four learning schemas. The identikit examines each schema as if it were a stand-alone. In keeping with what we have learned so far about the trilogy of the mind, each identikit refers to the learner's cognitive approach to processing information, conative mode of taking action, and affective source for developing a sense of self.

## Identikit One: The Sequential Processor

The sequential processor typically begins a learning task by asking, "What are the directions?" "What am I expected to do?" "Do you have an example I can look at?" "Can I see what students did last year?" (Meaning, "I don't want to start until I've seen a completed project that has met the teacher's expectations.")

My first reaction as a teacher was always, "Do you want to copy somebody else's work? What's wrong with you? Don't you have any ideas of your own?" I've learned that sequential processors are not going to copy anyone. They want the security of seeing what the whole project is supposed to look like. They want to make certain there are no hidden agendas. And they hate having the teacher change directions after they have started their work. Their security—their sense of self as a student—comes with, "I can do this well by using the techniques that have brought me success before. I will use them over and over."

Sequential processors need time to do their assignments carefully, methodically, neatly, and completely. They do not like to be rushed. If given enough time, they will double-check their answers. They also want to recopy their work for neatness before they submit it. You say, "Don't take time to recopy that," but because the neat appearance of their work represents them in a visible manner, they want to recopy it—they need to recopy it. They are the students who ask for late passes because it took them time to plan, organize, complete, and recheck their work.

Recently, I had a graduate student who began her 4-hour comprehensive exam by outlining her answer to each question in preparation for writing. Her outline was nine pages single spaced! It was so clearly organized with such specific subheadings that I would willingly have accepted her outline in lieu of the fully developed written responses. She, however, would never have gone along with that. First, to do that would be to submit an incomplete response to the test requirements. It would have interrupted her plan; it would have left her frustrated and concerned. She would not have been comfortable having me bend the rules for her.

Dalgliesh respected him [Kynaston] more than any other pathologist with whom he worked. He came promptly when called . . . and got down to his familiar routine. Soon, he knew, the two bodies would be neatly parcelled in plastic sheeting . . . the scene-of-the-crime exhibits packed, tagged, and carried to the police car.

—P. D. James, *A Taste for Death*, 1986, p. 75

Dalgliesh couldn't remember a piece of information from a witness more unwelcome . . . an unwelcome complication to his inquiry, a bizarre intrusion of irrationality into a job so firmly rooted in the search for evidence which would stand up in court, documented, demonstrable, real.

—P. D. James, *A Taste for Death*, 1986, p. 52

## Identikit Two: The Precise Processor

Precise processors typically begin cognitively processing an assignment by gathering a lot of data, a lot of facts, and a lot of specifics. Science teachers might term this an *atomistic* approach to gathering information. Precise processors are relentless in seeking information. They challenge you to provide more and more detail in your instruction. They want to know the source of your information. They are eager to share their knowledge of facts. They are frequently labeled "walking encyclopedias." They love trivia—sports stats, game shows, and Trivial Pursuit are their fare. They ask specific questions—lots of specific questions—until both classmates and you think, "Hey, give it a rest."

Precise processors take "really good notes." They gather information, memorize it, and prepare to demonstrate what they know through multiple choice tests or any test of fact. Precise processors do well on essays if given enough time to organize and report *all* that they know. One hazard of their knowing so many facts is that they do not always use their time wisely. They find themselves having answered one of three essays, albeit in great detail—in textbook fashion—but not able to answer the remaining questions because they have run out of time. Precise processors also enjoy researching information about topics of interest to them. They thrive on receiving written acknowledgments of their accomplishments—certificates, honor roll, or any record of fact.

Precise processors need information, act with precision, and feel good when the work is done exactly. My favorite precise processor story did not take place in a classroom. It took place in my living room, dining room, and front hallway. My husband, whose primary schema is precise processor, and I, whose primary schema is confluent processor, wallpapered our home. The wallpaper arrived Friday afternoon, and we needed to complete the job before holiday company arrived the next day.

I had all the equipment ready—the scissors, pans for soaking the paper, brushes, and so on. Secure in my preparation, I entered the living room with yardstick in hand, ready to measure the first length. What did I find? My husband was plumbing a line. Do you know what it means to plumb a line? It means "to establish a vertical line by hanging a plumb bob from a point near the corner of the room where the ceiling and wall meet." Okay. So, he plumbed a precise vertical line. Next, he measured the height of the wall. Then together we measured the wallpaper. Actually, we measured it twice. Then I cut it. And then my husband measured it again.

Now at this point, I think that once something is cut, it's over. He said he wanted to know if it was the right length. "Measure twice and cut once," he reminded me. "That is true, but the saying doesn't say 'measure again after you've cut!' " He said, "Well, I wanted to know if we did it right." I responded, "We'll know that when we paste it on the wall."

I had the terrible sensation that we would still be wallpapering when our guests came through the door the next day. It had taken us 30 minutes to do the first strip. We had the living room, the dining room, the stairwell, and the landing to do. I whined, "Do we have to measure everything three times? This could take all night." "How else would we do it?" he asked. "Well, we could eyeball the length we need and just cut it. The border will cover up any mistakes." He was not buying what I was selling.

My idea was, "Let's get movin'. Let's get it done and over with." "No, that's not how we do this. You have to measure if you're going to do it right." We were at a standstill, so I said, "How about we divide up the work. I'll do the living room. You do the dining room. Whoever gets through first goes on to the hallway." And that's what we did. He measured, measured, cut, and measured. I held up the roll, cut, and kept moving. We finished the job at 6:00 a.m. (Borders do cover a multitude of sins!)

This could also be called "A Tale of Two Schemas: Learning to Work Cooperatively."

## Identikit Three: The Technical Processor

Technical processors cognitively process information on an "as needed" basis. If information is extraneous, technical processors don't store it; they discard it. Information must be concise, to the point, and relevant to warrant their consideration. Relevance, real world, and rigor form their rationale for investing in any learning task. Without these validations, the task will be discounted or avoided altogether.

Technical processors are persons of few words. They write the shortest answers, the shortest paragraphs—only one draft of anything. And they believe what they put down represents much more than what the reader is actually able to find on the written page.

These learners understand tools, gadgets, and technical instruments. They speak their language. They think in operational terms. They like to "take things apart just to see what makes them tick . . . and put them back together without any leftover screws." A teacher overheard a 10-year-old technical processor talking to a buddy in class. One announced, "I got grounded." "Yeah? What for? What ya do?" "I took my mother's radio apart, but I couldn't quite get it back together. Then I tried the remote control!"

Technical processors seek opportunities to get physically involved in what they are doing. They don't want to read history from a book. They want to go to the battlefield where it happened. It is difficult for them to sit still in one place, in one row, in one position, class period after class period. These learners want a challenge—a mental and physical challenge.

Technical processors keep a physical and mental distance when they are involved in doing a challenging task. They prefer to work by themselves, thank you very much. "I don't really need or want you bending over my shoulder watching me do my work." In classrooms, they sit next to windows; they sit in the corner; they sit in the far back of the classroom. The more physical proximity you seek, the more they draw back.

She looked through GCSE Level A results. Very much as she'd expected. Costyn, K: Religious Education, "Unclassified"; English, "D"; Maths, "Unclassified"; Geography, "Unclassified"; Metalwork, "B." Well at least he'd got something—after twelve years of schooling . . . thirty six terms. But it was difficult to imagine him getting much further than the Job Centre. Nowhere else for him to go, was there—except . . .
—C. Dexter, *The Daughters of Cain,* 1994, p. 73

## Identikit Four: The Confluent Processor

The confluent processor begins processing information by asking, "What's this all about? How can I relate it to who I am? How can I play with it? Make it mine? Let me count the ways!" Consequently, it is the confluent processor who, in the middle of a focused activity, will say something totally unrelated. And your response as the teacher is, "Where did that come from?" Well, it came from within the learner. The confluent processor didn't get that descriptive name by remaining unconnected to life! Probably the learner saw something on television, or in a movie, or in a book, and now in the middle of your presentation, the learner sees a connection—a relationship that others in the class don't see.

Confluent processors use metaphors; they synthesize from all different areas of life and experience. They see the jointedness rather than the disjointedness of life. They thrive in settings in which integrated curricula are used. To the question "How would I have students learn?" one confluent learner responded, "By osmosis." That says it all. Jump in. Get into the middle of things. Absorb whatever is happening. That's how to learn.

Confluent processors won't follow the drill—they don't want directions *at all!* They rebel against what they believe are senseless rules. They thrive on change. One seventh grader told me, "My idea of the perfect school would be to have different teachers in different classrooms everyday. And no more stupid vocabulary books. I can't stand workbooks. Where's the creativity in them? They make me crazy!"

Confluent processors are whirlwinds of ideas looking for a place to touch down. Their hue and cry is "Let me have the freedom to run with this." They seek the freedom of self-expression. "I value my freedom to experiment, to use my own ideas and my own creative abilities."

I remember hearing a panel of writers, Lewis; and they said it was the most difficult thing finding a good title. Then one said she'd got half a dozen absolutely dazzling titles—she just hadn't got any books to go with them! And it's the same with me, I've got plenty of ideas already, but nothing to pin 'em to.
—C. Dexter, *The Daughters of Cain,* 1994, p. 40

## What Does This Look Like in the Classroom?

I observed a ninth-grade history class recently in which the students were to make a shield representing their family's history—land of origin, source of income, status in society, and so forth. The sequential processors designed their shields on paper and then organized all their materials before beginning. These students also cleaned their desktops and returned all materials to the teacher as soon as the warning bell rang.

The precise processors went back to their texts to check the definition of each of the terms that they were to represent. They then asked to be able to go to the library to use encyclopedias so they could verify the accuracy of the crests and flags of their ancestors' countries of origin.

The sole technical processor immediately went off by himself and began making the largest shield of all. He devoted his time to structuring the shield. Although he never arrived at the point of placing information on the shield, he had constructed his shield so well that it could have withstood the force of battle—any battle—or family reunion.

The confluent processors began working immediately, trying out their ideas and reflecting on their appearance as they went through one piece of "shield" paper after another. At the conclusion of class, a number of these students had not yet come upon a satisfactory representation, but the floor around their desks was strewn with interesting failed attempts.

For this lesson to be effective, the learners needed to understand how to make the best use of their individual schemas. They needed to know how to interact in a manner to produce a complete product representative of their pooled knowledge and talent. Part 4 of this text provides ideas for doing just that.

We need a Manhattan Project
to understand how a child
grows, learns, and develops.
—Boyer, 1993

# Interactive Learning Schemas

*The Good News and the Bad News*

## Interactive Learning Schemas Are Interactive (Good News)

**Our learning process consists of a pattern of patterns.**

Contradictory traits are not infrequently met in the same person.
—Allport, 1961, p. 390

The Interactive Learning Model is both simple and complex. Its simplicity lies in its four distinct schemas—each made up of the interaction of cognition, conation, and affectation. Therein, however, also lies its complexity. Each of these patterns operates within our interactive learning process at the same time! In other words, our learning process consists of a pattern of patterns.

It is not easy to picture the internal interaction of each schema simultaneously interacting with each of the other three schemas. A typo may have caused me to invent a new word to describe that interaction—"schemeshers."

Simple or complex, it is within this interaction that each person's individuality is found. It is in the unique mix of patterns within us that our will to learn is found. To unlock that will, therefore, we need to be able to answer the following: Which interactive pattern(s) do we choose to use first? Which is the one (or more) that we prefer not to use unless forced to do so? Which one(s) serves as a bridge between what we choose to use first and what we choose to use last? The answers to these questions form the basis of our learning combination!

*Learning Combination*

## Interactive Learning Schemas Are Multidimensional (More Good News)

As human beings, we are not one-dimensional; we are not two-dimensional; we are not three-dimensional. We are multidimensional. As learners, we have primary or "first choice of action" patterns and least preferred or "last choice" patterns. We also have schemas that lie somewhere between first and last on this imaginary continuum. The in-betweeners or bridge patterns are also important to who we are and how we learn.

My learning schema is a case in point. My first and foremost schema is confluent. My least used schema is sequential. In between are precise and technical. During my schooling, I used my precise schema more frequently than my technical. To whatever degree, however, I am all four schemas.

If you were to develop a profile of my interactive learning, you would first observe my use of confluence and then observe my lack of sequence. In the classroom, my confluent and sequential schema combination got on my teachers' nerves. Their most frequent comments were, "Oh! Now that's different," or "Can't you just do the assignment like I explained it?"

But that wasn't me. So, when I was given an assignment, I headed off in my own direction. I submitted projects that were different from what the teacher had envisioned. The two most unique were my popcorn shadowbox and my model of corduroy roads. The funniest was my attempt to fry an egg on dry ice. But failures didn't dampen my spirits. I was able to laugh at myself and my mistakes.

As a consequence of my many failed experiments, however, some teachers didn't take me seriously. When my petri dish grew wonderful purple crystals, the teacher refused to put my name on them even though he chose to display them at the spring science fair. He said no one would believe I had done such a sophisticated project. (He had not been impressed with my fried egg demo or my black-and-white photo display of fallout shelter signs.)

It was my bridge schema of precise processing that brought me my most positive feedback in the classroom. I could read, write, memorize, and take tests with the best of them. I just didn't do it unless I really had to—then I could. But it certainly was not my first choice for learning. My other bridge schema, technical processing, never appeared at all in the classroom. My brother would be the first to tell you that technical processing did not occur in the family garage, either. Although I worked as my brother's tool "gofer" when he repaired his '46 Ford coupe, his '56 Chevy, and his '61 Corvette, I never got the sense of what those tools were all about.

My technical processing took center stage for me in two other arenas—the kitchen and the sewing room. It has always been influenced and frequently upstaged by both my first and last choice schemas.

To this day, you can find me in the kitchen creating my own recipes—that's a part of my confluence. I look at the flavorings and

*Schemas*

*Sequential Processing*
Seeks clearer Directions. Needs time to plan. Thoroughly neat worker. Detailed

*Precise Processing*
Research + information. Writing as a Report. Trivia specialist concise writing

*Technical Processing*
Hands on builder Bored with lectures learns better IRC situations. Indepen. and private thinker Needs space to experiment

*Confluent Processing*
Beats to his own drum. Very creative and unique presenter uses multiple modalities of expression.

spices and I conjure them into any number of palatable items. Not following a recipe is the influence of my "avoid sequence and step-by-step directions." My technical processing involves my use of the tools of cookery. I know the instrument that works best when concocting sauces, fillings, gravies, or pastries. I like the feel of the pastry blender. I know the texture and consistency of the ingredients with which I am working.

I was raised by a mother who was a skilled seamstress, among other talents. She made all our clothes until I was well into high school. She made them by carefully following the pattern's directions; she attended to each detail—ripping and restitching until she had it exact. She taught me how to sew—how to use the Singer machine, the zipper foot, and the buttonhole maker—and how to cut against the grain and tear with the grain. She taught me the precise art of fitting a garment—how to construct darts and plackets, install zippers, match fabric patterns, and so on.

Once I had learned the basic procedures, however, I struck out on my own. I did not use a pattern. I scoffed at the idea. Instead, I spent my time imagining the product I wanted to create—a dress, a shirt, my wedding dress, the children's Halloween costumes, or in the latest instance, our granddaughter's baptismal gown. I would purchase the fabric and, after taking some basic measurements, simply cut the fabric into pieces that I knew would form whatever it was I was making.

That is how I use my patterned behaviors. I am first and foremost a confluent processor—and equally foremost, I avoid sequential processing. I am not devoid of sequence. I am not devoid of technical reasoning. I am not a minimalist when it comes to precision. More important, I am not deficient. I can use all four schemas when I have to. I operate most naturally, most comfortably, however, when I can use my "first choice" confluent processor. Just as I am me—uniquely me—as a human, as a learner, so each of us has an individual combination, and, with an understanding of our schemas, we can unlock our will to learn. We can make our combinations work for us!

## Interactive Learning Schemas Are Easily Misunderstood (Bad News)

The most misunderstood area of a learner is the schema the learner chooses to avoid using. Teachers and parents often misinterpret this part of the student's learning behavior as having a bad attitude or a "difficult" personality. What happens when the teacher does not recognize the student's least used schema? How does that affect the learning outcome? The rapport between teacher and student? I believe that misunderstandings of schemas occur from many different sources—teacher, parent, and student. When they do, they affect not only the classroom environment but, more important, the student's will to learn.

My daughter, who is not a precise processor, was taking instruction from her father and me on how to parallel park. I, a confluent processor,

took her into town, found a quiet side street, located a parked car behind which there were no other vehicles and said, "I am going to parallel park. Watch to see how far I pull up next to the vehicle, where I place my right arm, when I start to back in, and when I cut sharply to angle the final entrance into the parking spot."

Then I had her stand in front of the car and watch me as I again backed into the space. Finally, I said to her, "Here, you do it. I'll watch from outside; if you're too close to the other vehicle or if I think you might hit its bumper, I'll let you know. Otherwise, just keep practicing until you get the car fitted into the space; then do it three or more times until you feel confident about your judgment and movements."

For the next 30 minutes, I watched her maneuver and made encouraging comments when she succeeded, as succeed she eventually did. Then we moved down the street, and she rehearsed in the same manner, only this time parking between two vehicles.

That same afternoon, her father offered to help her practice. He parked our two cars out on our quiet residential street. At first he, too, stayed in the car directing her and commenting on her distance and timing. He was quickly relegated to observing from the lawn, where he continued to call out when and how to maneuver the vehicle.

Within 15 minutes, she was in the house, feigning a terrible headache and announcing, "Never let Dad teach me anything again." Her frustration arose, I believe, over the micromanagement of her training. Her father believed he was being helpful by announcing with precision the consequences of her every move. He sought to manage her learning experience precisely.

The two approaches were in conflict. Jane needed to discover and rehearse her sense of the complete flow of parking a vehicle; her dad needed to measure, gauge, and determine the exactness with which to make each turn. His well-meaning approach did not recognize that her avoidance of precise processing was a key component of her learning schema. His lack of awareness of this ultimately affected her will to learn under those circumstances.

Does knowing and understanding learning schemas make a difference for the learner? Does it make a difference in the teacher's effectiveness in facilitating learning? The previous example suggests that it does. Here are some other instances in which a lack of understanding of learning schemas may lead to a misinterpretation of a student's learning behavior. That misinterpretation then becomes translated into less than productive teacher-learner interactions in the classroom.

For example, if a learner uses sequential processing least, the teacher might view the learner as uncooperative—even rebellious. The teacher thinks, "This person doesn't have respect for organization." Or the teacher may discount the learner by thinking, "This student can't organize three peas in a pod! Look at that notebook, would you."

The fact is, this learner may not place any importance on neatness or organization. The student may feel stifled by directions and not see the value of following them. As one 9-year-old explained to the teacher, "Having to follow directions is like having you put your hand on my head and press down all the way to my feet." To write this person off as rebellious or uncooperative is to fail to understand the source of the behavior. It cuts off communication between learner and teacher. It replaces learning with false accusation and misguided criticism. (Part 3 of the text provides insights into how to avoid misinterpretations of this sort.)

If learners use the precise schema least, they are frequently perceived as not knowing the answers. When you call on those students, you feel they are never able to "pin the answer down." To you, they seem to have a vague sense of what the answer is all about, but they don't use much specific information—names or dates. The students don't answer by using the precise terminology you want to hear. The teacher or parent may surmise that the learners have been lazy and just haven't put forth the effort or taken the time to memorize these important facts.

For the learners who use the precise schema least, the specificity of the information is not important. They don't invest in attending to or logging detailed information into their long-term memory. They *can* do it if they have to. They *will* do it when it is vital to them. A good example of this is the inane information students will memorize to pass their driver's test. The learners will absorb the necessary information, retain it long enough to spit it back, and then discharge it from their memory, labeling it as unnecessary information that is just "cluttering up the brain!"

Learners who use their technical processing schema least do not experience as much negative feedback in the school setting as do learners who use their sequential, precise, or confluent least. Because there are so few learning settings provided whereby this schema is observed or required in the classroom, students are rarely observed shirking opportunities to use technical reasoning or technical problem solving. The science labs, technology labs (shops), and some art classes may be the exceptions.

Although learners who avoid technical processing may not choose to operate power tools or build structures, they may demonstrate technical skill through computer wizardry or basic trial and error. They will learn to fix the tracking on the VCR and handle basic daily technological challenges when life requires them to do so. But they do not choose to make their living in this manner!

If learners are least willing to take risks, they may incorrectly be labeled unimaginative or uncreative (lacking creativity). These learners are not dull or unresponsive simply because they take time to mull or carefully think through how they want to do an assignment. They are not slow. They are deliberate. These learners do not thrive when given "quick quizzes" or when required to brainstorm.

There are also many instances in which they will get moving rapidly on an activity because they *do* know the procedures—they've been there before—the territory is familiar. Their originality lies in their use of their dominant schema or schemas, not in the schema that requires risks where they have had no experience. These learners want

Interestingly many schools reward different types of learning in different grades. Detail-oriented, verbal learners succeed in the early grades. Analytic, big-picture problem solvers do better in the latter grades. Think-on-your-feet type problem solvers do best in the real world . . . but how many of these learners become so discouraged because they are seen as slow-reading, weak students that they give up their intellectual goals long before their learning strengths are realized?
—Greenspan & Lodish, 1991, p. 307

assurance that what they have in mind will be accepted. This doesn't mean they can't be creative. It simply means that this is an area they would not choose to operate out of on a daily basis. It isn't natural for them; it is stressful. They don't like being pushed off a cliff and being told they can fly.

There is one more twist on the problem of "seeing" and misinterpreting a learner's schema. Some learning schemas appear to the student to be valued more by the teacher than others—they please the teacher more. The youngest of students is capable of observing this but is not able to discern why. This leads to some interesting conclusions by the student and bewilderment on the part of the teacher. If the young learner sees another learner's schema receiving positive feedback from the teacher, the learner may attempt to conform to that same behavior even though it doesn't feel right or even work well for the student.

I had a 9-year-old student once who asked question after question—the answers to which had less and less to do with anything of significance to the topic. At one point, he complained to his mother that I wouldn't call on him when he had his hand up and that I wouldn't answer his questions.

When the mother and child sat down with me to discuss the situation, we learned that he thought asking questions was a sign of intelligence. His cousin, who was in the same class, was considered very bright by the family, and she always asked a lot of questions. He wanted to appear bright, so he began asking questions, too. What he did not realize was that his cousin's primary learning schema was precise processing. Her questions, although many in number, were specific and sought to establish an in-depth understanding of the focus of the lesson. They were topic-relevant. The reason he did not get the opportunity to ask question after question was that his questions were off-topic and distracting—especially because of their mindless and disconnected nature. This student was mimicking the outward, conative behaviors of a precise processor without understanding the cognitive or affective aspects of the schema. The motivation to do this was affectively induced. "I want recognition. Teachers recognize questioners. I'll become a questioner."

Greenspan & Lodish, 1991

I will address this type of reaction of a student-learner more completely in Part 3. I simply want to make the point that we all can misinterpret learning schemas.

## Interactive Learning Schemas Come in All Forms (Good News)

I must confess that I came into this schema thing having first spent a good deal of my teaching time looking at the student through the lenses of learning styles. I saw one student as an intuitive feeler, another as a concrete analyst, so forth and so on. For me, that meant that using data or information was done by only one type of learner;

doing hands-on was done only by another. Once I understood the dynamic of the interactive schema, I recognized that information or autonomy or hands-on projects are not the exclusive functions of individual schemas but have a role in all schemas. All the schemas do all these in their own unique manner!

They each exhibit cognitive, conative, and affective behaviors in keeping with the sequential, precise, technical, or confluent nature of their schemas! Below are just a few of the ways our multitude of behaviors manifest themselves within each of our unique interactive learning schemas:

### Information Processing

- Sequential processors process information by organizing it and summarizing it.
- Precise processors process information by collecting, analyzing, and questioning it.
- Technical processors process information by looking for relevance and jettisoning meaningless information.
- Confluent processors process information by sifting it to find a unique perspective.

### Autonomy

- Sequential processors develop their *own* system of information storage and retrieval.
- Precise processors accumulate their *own* information, find it, verify it, and check the accuracy themselves.
- Technical processors have their *own* way of taking charge; they analyze the givens, do trial and error, and just "get the job done."
- Confluent processors use their *own* ideas. They follow their imaginations; they thrive on doing things out of the ordinary—never before tried.

### Hands-On

- Hands-on for sequential processors means doing something other than paper and pencil. Hands-on means watching a video and doing a discussion following a preset list of questions; it means doing a scavenger hunt—again completing the work by locating each item on a list.
- Hands-on for precise processors involves reading primary sources—diaries, journals, and letters—not encyclopedias. It means going to a museum and finding out information firsthand on-site! It means surfing the Internet and finding the information

themselves. It means doing a lab that involves precise measurements and recording of results.

- Hands-on for technical processors means using technical equipment or building something—as one student expressed it, "Not like building a log cabin with Lincoln logs—really building something!" Hands-on means building the set and designing the mechanisms by which scenery changes flawlessly during a school production.

- Hands-on for confluent processors means doing a skit; extemporaneously role playing; doing an art project; and designing, painting, and sculpting.

## Interactive Learning Schemas Can Be Learner Friendly (the Best News)

We can grow in our ability to learn. That is what the learner-centered classroom is all about—but we need to know what we are as individual learners and how to enhance and use our schemas to the best learning advantage. Relying on generalized descriptions, painting broad-stroke representations, or ascribing a label to a student is not the answer to understanding a learner's will to learn. Remember, we are a *pattern of patterns*. The degree to which we use each of these is what makes us unique as individual learners. Seeking to understand each part of a learner's combination of schemas is the key to unlocking each learner's will to learn. To do that, we need a means to capture the learner's interactive schema—we need an instrument that can do this. That is why the *Learning Combination Inventory* was developed. And that is what Part 3 of the text is all about.

# 3

# FINDING THE COMBINATION

## As We Continue

Up to this point, our recognition of the patterns that make up an individual's interactive learning process has relied on examining student work-product and student voices. Now it is time to examine a standardized means of doing this, as we seek to find the combination that unlocks the learner's chamber of personal learning energy. Before you begin this section, you will want to complete and score the Learning Combination Inventory found in Appendix A.

The completion of the LCI is a very important step. It is the beginning of a process. The process involves the learner and the teacher in capturing the learner's pattern of learning schemas, establishing a dialogue, and formulating strategies to use both inside and outside the classroom. Part 3 explains how the teacher and the learner can share in the opportunity and the challenge of *Unlocking the Will to Learn.*

*LCI =*

*Learning*
*Combination*
*Inventory*

# 11

I do what I do because I think, "That's how I'm me." That's when I'm secure as a learner.
—D. Johnston, personal communication, February 17, 1995

# The Lock, the Learner, and the Combination

## The Lemon Law

How would you shop for a car? What would you look for? Price. Style. Color. Gas mileage. Projected cost of insurance. Trade-in value. Safety features. Would you get some ideas first? Read *Consumer Reports?* Talk to a friend who already owns the model you are looking for? Call your brother-in-law for advice? Go to the only dealer in town?

You may think I'm leading up to explaining what type of learner would do each of the above. Actually, we did that quite extensively in Part 2. In Part 3, we are going to examine the Learning Combination Inventory, an instrument for collecting information about a learner's combination of learning schemas. The point of introducing the chapter in this manner is simply to draw attention to the fact that when we go out to purchase a major investment on which we need to depend for some time, we take our time and choose carefully. The same should be true when we look for an instrument to help us understand how a learner learns.

## Practicing What We've Preached

This book has held up as important several issues concerning the learner and the learning process. These issues form the integrity of the

Interactive Learning Model. They should also form the basis of any instrument used to gather information about the learner. This then becomes the charge:

The instrument must

- Have the learner at its center
- Look at the learner as a whole—at the learner's cognitive, conative, and affective processing
- Provide insights into the learner's motivation—the learner's will
- Capture the individual's pattern of learning patterns

## How Does the Learning Combination Inventory Measure Up?

The Learning Combination Inventory is a natural way to begin the process of unlocking the student's will to learn. From the outset, however, we need to understand that the inventory itself is only a paper-and-pencil instrument—it is not the process. The process involves much more. It includes the learner and teacher engaging in conversations about how accurately the inventory describes the learner. It continues with the learner and teacher discussing how to apply the insights gained from the learner-teacher dialogues. The Learning Combination Inventory initiates the process, but it is not the end product. It is a means, not an end. It is only a tool, only one step in unlocking the will to learn.

The Learning Combination Inventory begins with two introductory paragraphs that set the tone for the remainder of the process. We recognize here an interest in and concern for the learner beyond what can be represented by a numerical score alone.

Your teachers and parents have probably told you many times that learning is an important part of life. Something they may not have told you is that we all learn in different ways. Each one of us has his or her own special learning combination. It is this combination that helps us think and understand, work and perform, and develop and mature as capable, successful persons.

Your thoughtful answers to the following questions can help your teacher and you understand what your learning combination is. Please read each sentence carefully and respond to it as accurately as you can. If you have a question while completing this inventory, please ask your teacher to help you.

## Unlocking the Lock: How Does It Work?

The Learning Combination Inventory (LCI) is a 28-item self-report scale that can be administered to an entire classroom of students or one-on-one, depending on the learner's reading and writing level. Two forms of the inventory have been developed: one for use with elementary students and the other for use with high school through college-age students. The inventory consists of two parts. The first part has 28 descriptive sentences that the learner reads and then indicates how the statements relate to him or her—"never ever," "almost never," "sometimes," "almost always," and "always" on a 5-point Likert-type scale. The second part consists of three parallel question stems. The inventory indicates the learner's use of the following four schemas: sequential processor, precise processor, technical processor, and confluent processor.

More than 4,500 students in 37 public, private, and parochial districts, including 20 national and 5 international sites, participated in the instrument's development. The Learning Combination Inventory is designed to measure the multidimensional nature of learning: the cognitive, conative, and affective interaction discussed in Parts 1 and 2 of this text.

During a 3-year period, the coauthor of the LCI and I spent hundreds of hours interviewing students and teachers, observing classes, and collecting data. From this, we cataloged students' descriptions of their learning behaviors. This information led to the development of a 64-item pilot instrument. The factorial analysis of these data, the verification of findings through subsequent interviews of previous participants, and the conducting of additional analyses resulted in a 28-item/three-sentence stem instrument we call the Learning Combination Inventory.

## Identifying the Combination

The LCI is a self-report instrument. It doesn't test a quality; it doesn't determine the capacity to learn; it doesn't measure what the learner knows. The inventory reports what learners selected as descriptions of their learning behaviors. It inventories. It takes stock. It identifies the *what* and *how much* of each schema. It is as accurate as the person who reports it is willing to make it. It doesn't diagnose what is wrong. It doesn't prescribe how to increase an area of deficiency. It simply tallies what is there. It invites learners to express their thoughts on what frustrates them about assignments, how they prefer to show what they know, and how they would have students

**Figure 11.1.**

Name_____ Teacher_____

**Part I.**

**Reminder:** This is not a test. It is a way to find out about how you accomplish learning tasks. Below are 28 statements each followed by five phrases that indicate how the statement might relate to you—"never ever," "almost never," "sometimes," "almost always," and "always." These phrases are numbered from one to five.

**Directions:** Here is what you are to do. 1) Read each sentence carefully. 2) Decide how well it fits what you do to learn. 3) Circle the numbered phrase that matches your response. 4) Write the number you have circled on the line to the left of the statement. 5) Be sure that you circle only one phrase for each statement.

**Let's practice!**

**Sample Statements:**

_____ A. I listen carefully when the teacher is giving directions.

| 1 | 2 | 3 | 4 | 5 |
|---|---|---|---|---|
| NEVER EVER | ALMOST NEVER | SOME-TIMES | ALMOST ALWAYS | ALWAYS |

_____ B. I like to stand in the front of the class and act out skits or plays.

| 1 | 2 | 3 | 4 | 5 |
|---|---|---|---|---|
| NEVER EVER | ALMOST NEVER | SOME-TIMES | ALMOST ALWAYS | ALWAYS |

**Words of Encouragement:** Remember, this is **not** a test! So, take all the time you need, and do the very best you can. Have fun, relax, and enjoy learning more about yourself.

**Figure 11.2.**

It is a self-report instrument. It places the learner center stage by assigning the learner the lead role and by giving the teacher the supporting role.

It uses a Likert-type scale. It gives the learner the opportunity to consider the choices, embrace them, accept them, or reject them.

It uses open-ended questions. It listens to the learner. It doesn't force answers on the learner; it allows the learner to present or divulge his or her thoughts on the subject of learning.

A true dialogue does not aim at persuading the other one, nor deluding him, nor simply dumbfounding him. We enter into dialogue in order to find something out together.
—Sallstrom, 1991, p. 28

learn if they were teachers. The LCI, by its very format, invites learners to report the patterns of their learning process.

Because the LCI is part of a process, the interpretation of the outcome takes place *after* the inventory is completed, not before—it is generated from the student's expression, not predetermined by a set of numbers or a "one size fits all" set of canned descriptors. The LCI uses the student's own thoughts—written expressions—as the basis of the interpretation—and it is not complete without these!

By interpreting the results of the LCI in light of who the learner is, rather than interpreting the learner on the basis of normed results, the learner and the teacher can use the results of the LCI to carry on substantive conversations about how the learner learns. The instrument and teacher aren't telling the learner what the learner is; the information provided by the LCI is confirming for the learner what the learner already knows but may not know how to express. It is a declaration to teacher and parents:

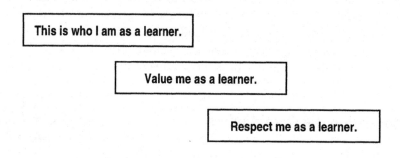

This is who I am as a learner.

Value me as a learner.

Respect me as a learner.

## On Becoming a Locksmith

Because the purpose of this instrument is to begin a learner-teacher dialogue, the activities that follow the student's completion of the inventory are used to open the lines of communication—to establish a dialogue—and to create an atmosphere in which the learner can negotiate learner-specific strategies for adapting his or her pattern of schemas to the learning requirements.

Remember, the student's learning combination consists of a number of tumblers (the patterns of how you know, act, and feel) that need to be carefully identified and discussed if the student and the teacher are going to be able to appreciate and respect the complexity and uniqueness of the student's learning combination.

The learning combination is first reported in a sequence of scores for each schema. The mix of tumblers is represented as the student's learning combination. The first digit represents a learner's tendency to use sequential processing, the second precise processing, the third technical processing, and the fourth confluent processing. Note that the combination is divided into ranges for each of the four schemas. Each range of the LCI indicates the extent to which a student chooses to use a schema first, to use a schema as needed, or to avoid a certain schema when completing a learning task. These numbers are then represented visually on the bar graphs below the rows of minilocks.

The student's learning combination is further described in the student's written answers. To interpret these, turn to the chart of sample written responses (Appendix A) and locate phrases or expressions similar in wording or intent to those found on the student's answer sheet. Note under which schema the responses are located. You will want to discuss to what extent these match the individual's numerical scores for each schema.

At this point in the process, the teacher assumes the responsibility of listening-clarifying to confirm the consistency of the student's responses on the LCI. To accomplish this, the teacher needs to be secure in interpreting the student's written responses. For some readers, what follows may appear redundant. For others, it may serve to reinforce their understanding of the schema descriptors presented in Part 2.

For example, a student whose numerical scores are high in sequential processing might write responses similar to the following: "Assignments are frustrating when they aren't thoroughly explained," or "When I'm not given enough information about an assignment and am then told I've done it wrong." The written responses are often done in outline form or as a list of items set off by a dash or an asterisk.

A student whose numerical scores are high in precise processing might write, "I prefer to demonstrate my knowledge by answering essay questions or writing a paper." "If I were the teacher, I would have students read, take notes, and demonstrate their understanding by essay or a verbal demonstration." The precise processor's written responses may also be identified through wordiness, thoroughness, and exactness. Answers often spill over the borders of the designated space, indicating the student's need to record all that the student deems important to prove his or her knowledge to the teacher.

A student whose numerical scores show technical processing as the dominant first choice may most frequently

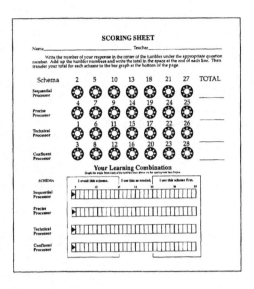

**Figure 11.3.**

The score for each of the scales needs to be carefully analyzed to determine the degree to which these numbers represent the learner. If you don't do that, you violate the process.

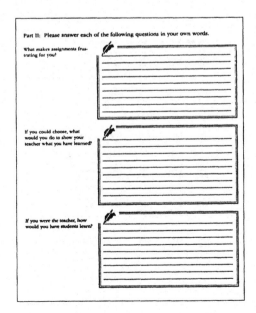

**Figure 11.4.**

Quite likely, some learning strategies are readily learned for use in appropriate situations whereas others are manifestations of deep-seated ability or personality structures.
—Snow & Jackson, 1992, p. 89

describe "not wanting to be here." "I hate doing things that make no sense. What's the purpose?" "I would teach by letting students learn in their own way." "Let them get out into the real world." "Take us to see how things really work. Not learning from a book." These learners tend to use the fewest words or sentences to state their answers.

A student whose numerical scores on the four schemas indicate a strong tendency to use confluent processing may write, "I don't want to be forced to do an assignment in only one way." "I would like to see teachers present lessons and material in a variety of ways." "I would prefer to get up and do a skit." "Give an oral presentation."

## Listening for the Click of the Tumblers: 24-30-9-15

For those who want to see the numbers and hear the click of the lock's combination from the beginning to the end of the process, I have written a step-by-step scenario. Of course, the place to begin is with the student's responses to the 28 LCI statements. You will want to guide the student in transferring the individual "tumbler" answers to the actual LCI Scoring Sheet. Here, for the first time, you will learn the combination of the patterns that appear to form this learner's interactive process (24-30-9-15). Once you have used these numbers and colored in the bar graph at the bottom of the Scoring Sheet, you can begin your discussion with the learner. You will want to do so by referring to the schema that the student chooses to use most frequently.

In this case, you would seek to determine if this learner sees him- or herself processing and performing school learning tasks in a precise, detailed manner. Actually, this learner will probably engage you through question and answer, asking the meaning of all these numbers—specifically as each pertains to him or her. The score of 30 out of a possible 35 indicates that this learner uses all aspects of the precise processing schema equally.

Remember, even if the numerical score appears conclusive, do not forget to read and discuss the learner's written responses. These can be used to expand on the learner's Likert responses—to further confirm their accuracy or to clarify the extent of their influence on the student's learning combination.

Next, you should check to see if this learner can confirm for you that the learner does not choose to use the technical processing schema unless forced to do so. Discussing the score of 9 in that schema may require good listening skills because this student explains in detailed terms some of the assignments or learning experiences that she or he has avoided or completed without great success. That leaves the two "use as needed" schemas—the 24 in sequential processing and the 15 in confluent processing.

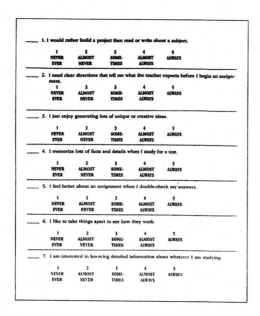

**Figure 11.5.**

Both of these fall into the bridging category, yet each is located at the opposite end of the midrange of the continuum. What does that mean? It means that you need to converse further with the learner to discover what part of each of these schemas the learner uses and with what consistency.

For example, in sequential processing, does the student want clear, step-by-step directions? Does the student seek an example to follow when completing an assignment or project? Although the answers to these questions may be "yes," the answer to the learner's concern about neatness and double-checking answers might be, "That isn't me at all." This is valuable information that the numerical score of 24 does not reveal. Only a discussion with the student can pinpoint the *pattern within the pattern* that the learner uses.

The 15 in confluent processing is also important to discuss. Again, reviewing which aspects of confluence the learner uses more frequently than others is vital to understanding the student's learning behaviors.

Finally, you will want to review the written responses once again from a more holistic perspective. In doing this, you are likely to find that the student frequently has written about the learner's most used and most strongly avoided schemas—and will do so in a manner that shows how, within the learner, these opposites have the greatest effect on the learner's behavior. For example, a learner whose combination is 28-19-21-7 might write, "I am most frustrated when the teacher doesn't give clear directions." (This reflects the score of 28.) "I don't like having to come up with my own ideas." (This reflects the score of 7.) "I'd rather know exactly what's expected of me." (Again, this reflects the 28 of sequential processing.)

In this case, the written response confirms both schemas—sequential and confluent. From this, both the learner and the teacher have gained an understanding of the learner's preference to perform and preference to avoid certain learning situations.

What if the learning combination does not indicate a dominant choice to use a certain schema first or does not result in a score that reveals a dominant "I choose this last" schema? Does this mean the learner has no pattern? Should we interpret that the learner has no preference for one schema of learning over another? The answer is, "no" and "no." If a learner's scores all fall within the bridge range or the "I can use these as needed," then that constitutes the learner's pattern. Before drawing this conclusion, however, complete the LCI process to determine which aspects of each schema this learner scored as "I avoid" and which the learner scored as "I choose first." Remember, within each schema is a set of responses and behaviors that compose the overall schema. Therefore, it is essential that the learner

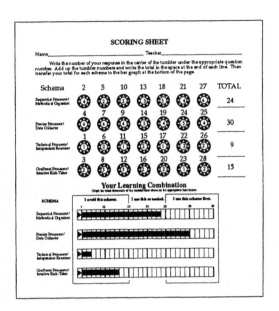

**Figure 11.6.**

### Patterns Within Patterns

Sequential Processors
*Seeker of Clear Directions*
*Practiced Planner*
*Thoroughly Neat Worker*
*(methodical, neat, complete)*
Precise Processors
*Information Specialist*
*Into-Details Researcher*
*Answer Specialist*
*Report Writer*
*(data, details, questions)*
Technical Processors
*Hands-On Builder*
*Independent/Private Thinker*
*Reality Seeker*
*(concise, relevant, real)*
Confluent Processors
*Different Drummer*
*Creative Imaginer*
*Unique Presenter*
*(creative, intuitive, risk-taking)*

and the teacher explore these to gain an understanding of this student's "balanced" pattern of patterns.

Before we move to Chapter 12, I stress again that the Learning Combination Inventory is a self-report instrument. Use this step of the LCI process to find out why the learner reported what she or he did. That means *you* need to listen, and the *learner* needs to talk. This is where the learner begins unlocking the will to learn; this is where the teacher begins to understand how to facilitate this process—not outside the learning circle thumbing through a technical manual of psychometric interpretations—but here within the learning arena, putting the learner once again at the center.

Once you have reviewed the makeup of each pattern and discussed the learning combination these form, it is time to move to the next step in the LCI process—discussing how to use the learning combination in a manner that unlocks the student's will to strive to achieve an array of learning goals.

---

**The Goals of the Learning Combination Inventory Process**

- To help students become aware of their learning combinations and to appreciate their uniqueness as learners
- To teach students how to negotiate learning tasks once they know their learning combinations
- To teach students how to develop strategies for learning tasks that do not fit comfortably within their learning combinations
- To teach students how to work with others and to appreciate their unique learning combinations
- To teach students how to develop and mature as confident learners who recognize their aptitudes and performance traits and know how to use them to build stronger and healthier senses of self

---

**Box 11.1.**

# 12

We have kids who don't know their learning schemas because we haven't allowed them to explore those schemas. And we have students who know their schemas but have not been allowed to develop them.
—Elementary guidance counselor, personal communication, February 20, 1995

# If I Don't Like My Numbers, Can I Trade Them In?

## Teacher, I Can't Get My Combination to Work

I continue to be surprised at the number of learners who believe that the Learning Combination Inventory has captured their learning patterns accurately but who just don't want to be that pattern! They want to be more technical, less sequential, more this, or more that. Of course, these learners raise an important question: "If I don't like my numbers, can I trade them in?" I remember asking that question each fall right after I found out where my locker was located or who my locker partner was going to be. But the question of changing our learning combination is of a much more serious nature than the social incompatibility of locker partners.

In Part 2, we reviewed the well-established belief that our systems of thought, language, and behavior consist of a pattern of patterns, patterns that are stable through time. This is called our self-stability. Those who have studied learning behaviors have suggested that we may have three types of learning tendencies—inherent, synthetic, and adopted-artificial, which never becomes part of our typical functioning. Although not subject to fundamental change, these patterns are subject to modification.

Witkin, 1978

Bandura, 1977

Gregorc & Ward, 1977

Keefe & Ferrell, 1990

Riessman, 1964

Learning theorists believe that our schemas are not so prescriptive that we can't alter them. We can grow and change, but we need to know what our schemas are and how to enhance and use them to the best learning advantage.

We also need to be realistic. Those parts of our patterns that are dominant are the ones we alter the least. It is these that are the most painful and frustrating to alter, ignore, or tone down for an extended time. We can alter any one of our schemas when we absolutely must. Left to our own devices, however, through time these altered behaviors will return to the original comfort zone of patterned behaviors. We don't have the same sense about using them as we do our first-choice schemas.

*Most behaviors are under the control of processes that are not altered by any present stimuli.*
—Powers, 1989, p. 24

## Right Pattern; Wrong Situation

STOP, DROP, ROLL?
*or*
RUN HOME FAST?

We don't always use our learning patterns to our advantage; that is, we don't always match them to the situation at hand in the most effective manner. Here I think of the graduate student who told the story of a child who was accosted by a stranger on the way home from school. She began, "We had a 9-year-old student who was walking home from school when a man drove up beside him on the street, rolled down the car window, and attempted to convince the child to come into the car. The child's response was to stop, drop, and roll."

I suppose it was a bit of a shock to see the little boy suddenly disappear from view, hit the ground, and begin to roll back and forth. The point is that the child had learned the patterned response of what to do in case his clothes were to catch on fire. He had just finished fire prevention month at school, and the child clearly had this pattern of behavior down! What the child did not have down was when to use that behavior appropriately. Two months prior to this incident, the children at his school had met a police officer who taught them never to talk with strangers, never to take candy from a stranger, and never to get into a stranger's car. Well, the little boy had learned both patterns of how to deal with danger but did not know when to use each appropriately.

This may be true with our schemas, also. We need to learn how and when to use each one. Not only do many students not know how or when to use their learning schemas to their advantage, but teachers frequently do not know how to help students make the match. All too often, teachers observe certain behaviors and respond negatively to learners' requests because they believe what they are observing are avoidance behaviors and what they are hearing are excuses from students. Teachers fail to understand that these behaviors may well be the students' efforts to negotiate what they need to be successful as learners. Listed below by learning schema are a set of requests that a teacher might hear from a student whose first choice of schema is sequential, precise, technical, or confluent.

As an important part of the LCI process, you will need to review these requests and identify which of them the student-learner most frequently uses. When viewed in this manner, the student's requests may be better understood by the teacher and accepted as legitimate bases on which to negotiate a response beneficial to the learner and acceptable within the learning context.

## How and When to Negotiate the Learning Environment

### Sequential Processor Tumblers

If the learner's first-choice schema is sequential processor, it is reasonable to expect that the learner will ask the teacher for

- A review of the directions
- A sample to see or read over
- Time to develop an outline/plan
- More time to do the assignment
- Extra time to double-check answers and to make corrections if errors are found
- Time to recopy for neatness

### Precise Processor Tumblers

If the learner's first-choice schema is precise processor, it is reasonable to expect that the learner will ask the teacher for

- Time to check the accuracy of recorded information and the spelling of names and places
- Time to look up additional information to verify the correctness and completeness of the information given in class
- Assurance that what was heard and recorded in the student's notes was accurate
- An explanation of facts, dates, and events as proof of knowledge and as a means of providing a context and relevance to the information

### Technical Processor Tumblers

If the learner's first-choice schema is technical processor, it is reasonable to expect that the learner will ask the teacher to

- Be left alone while working
- Be allowed to attempt varying projects in lieu of writing or doing paper-and-pencil assignments

- Be permitted to construct projects and objects to show the learner's skills
- Be the group manager of group assignments
- Be able to use mechanical ability in completing assignments

### Confluent Processor Tumblers

If the learner's first-choice schema is confluent processor, it is reasonable to expect that the learner will ask the teacher to

- Be allowed to begin the assignment and ask for directions later as needed
- Be permitted to do the assignment in a unique manner
- Withhold discouraging criticism as a variety of novel ideas are generated
- Be permitted to start over with another idea
- Receive early and frequent feedback on a novel approach to doing the assignment
- Be allowed to present an original skit, speech, or public performance of some type

## How and When to Use Strategies to Adapt to the Learning Environment

There will be times when negotiation is not possible. At such times, the student will need to adopt a strategy as a guide in the successful completion of the learning task. Again, as a part of the process-through-time, the teacher will need to discuss and build on the following sets of strategies to determine which will work best for the student.

### Scenario 1

A learner whose first-choice learning schema is **sequential processor** has been given an assignment in a hurried manner without clear directions and/or without any examples provided. What can this learner do to survive?

When the directions aren't clear or complete,

- Recall a previous assignment that required the same outcome.
- Think through the steps you used to complete that assignment.
- Give yourself several minutes to list what steps you completed that made you successful.

When there is no time to double-check all answers,

- Put a star by those answers to which you need to return to double-check.

When there is no time to recopy for corrections or neatness,

- Write your response as deliberately as possible. Come prepared to use a pencil and eraser or a pen with erasable ink as needed. Use arrows, numbers, and clear-line cross-outs to correct and edit your work. You may want to learn four or five standard editorial abbreviations to use to note changes you would make if time permitted. These markings suggest you are aware of changes that would strengthen your answer if you were to have an opportunity to resubmit or recopy the assignment.
- Tell yourself that you are submitting the assignment in as neat a form as possible under the circumstances.

## Scenario 2

A learner whose first-choice learning schema is **precise processor** has been given an assignment after only a brief and incomplete explanation. The key information needed to complete the assignment was not provided. What can this learner do to survive?

When lectures or directions are incomplete,

- Read through your notes or the assignment to see if you can answer questions you have about missing or unclear information.
- Write down questions on a separate piece of paper that you need to ask the teacher before or after class.
- Use dates and events to corroborate your understanding of the information.

When there isn't enough time to answer questions completely,

- Start your answers with the most important information and then fill in the blanks.
- List the information you know to show that you have knowledge of it; outline it if possible.
- Prioritize your use of time. Answer the questions with the greatest point value first.

## Scenario 3

A learner whose first-choice learning schema is **technical processor** has been given an assignment requiring the student to work in a cooperative learning group doing a paper-and-pencil assignment. What can this learner do to survive?

When there is little or no autonomy,

- Decide what role you have and stick to it.
- Think of others as advisers who are there to help you.
- Use teachers for their knowledge; do not think of them as only authority figures.

When there are few hands-on assignments,

- Design a strategy to complete the assignment in a manner that gives it relevance to your life.
- Take a 10-minute break after every 30 minutes of work.
- Stay focused on what needs to be completed. Don't let your mind wander to other things you'd rather be doing.

When there is little or no technical ability required to complete an assignment,

- Break the assignment down into sections, completing one section at a time.
- Turn the assignment into a game, timing yourself or seeing how many problems you can do in a certain amount of time.
- Complete the task in school so that you can do the things you like to do after school.

### Scenario 4

A learner whose first-choice learning schema is **confluent processor** has been given an assignment requiring the student to sit through a lengthy explanation of procedures and requiring that a single set of procedures be followed in a timely manner to produce a particular product. What can the learner do to survive?

When the teacher is taking a long time to explain the directions,

- Look at the assignment sheet and underline key words, dates, and features of the assignment. (This will help you focus on what is being explained.)
- Think of questions to ask that demonstrate your interest and attention to what is being explained.
- Remember a time when not following directions caused a loss of time and achievement on the assignment.
- Stay focused.

When no one has time to listen to your ideas,

- Write down the ideas in a special place and talk to someone about them later.

When there is no opportunity to use unique or different ways of doing the assignment,

- Think about what is to be learned by doing the assignment in the manner required by the teacher.
- Do the assignment in two different ways: the way it was assigned and a novel or unique way; submit both for credit.

When there is no time to do an oral presentation in class,

- Plan an oral presentation and make a videotape of it; submit it to the teacher and ask for feedback.

## General Strategies for Enhancing Each Tumbler of Your Learning Combination

There will also be times when the learner will be required to use an adopted-artificial learning scheme—one that is *not* a preferred learning scheme for the student. It may even be foreign to the learner. I am referring here to being required to use a schema that the student not only prefers not to use but also has little or no idea of how to begin to use.

When such an instance occurs, both the learner and the teacher need to be prepared to discuss what general strategies the learner can use as a guide in completing the task. This is the ultimate test of the learner-teacher dialogue. It is the pivotal point of making the LCI process viable and educationally enhancing for the student-learner. To arrive at this point and to overcome the challenge can have a long-lasting and positive effect on the learner's will to learn. Effort that is focused and appropriately directed toward a task can make the learning experience truly positive. Not attending to this can result in an equally negative experience for the learner. Here is a set of strategies to use. The learner and teacher will need to determine which will work best in a given situation.

If you *avoid* **sequential processing,** but your class assignments require that you use it, here are some tips for adjusting your combination to succeed one assignment at a time.

- Don't start an assignment before you know what is expected of you. Determine the focus or point of the assignment and stick to it.

Adapting characteristics so as to equip the learner is clearly a training goal of preference.
—Witkin & Goodenough, 1982, p. 63

- Think of each assignment as having a beginning, a middle, and an end. Then approach the assignment in that manner, checking your progress at each of the three points.
- Schedule your school day and afterschool time to allow you to complete the work that is required.
- Plan whenever possible. Plan how you want to do the assignment, what you want to write, how you want to answer questions, and what your key thoughts are; then begin the assignment.
- Allow for sufficient time to complete and double-check answers on assignments or tests.

If you *avoid* **precise processing,** but your class assignments require that you use it, here are some tips for adjusting your combination to succeed one assignment at a time.

- Don't trust your memory; write down times, events, and schedules.
- Study by practicing answering questions using specific dates and events.
- Use the process of elimination or deduction rather than guessing at answers.
- Save old assignments and tests for future use.
- Write questions to ask the teacher on a separate piece of paper as you are taking notes.
- Use questions of classmates to gain an understanding of why certain information is important and how the pieces of information relate to one another.

If you *avoid* **technical processing,** but your class assignments require that you use it, here are some tips for adjusting your combination to succeed one assignment at a time.

- Analyze why things work the way they do.
- Take simple things apart to see what is inside.
- Plan your days and weeks so that you have time for physical activity.
- Plan to spend time by yourself doing what you enjoy most.
- Remain focused on any task you are working on.

If you *avoid* **confluent processing,** but your class assignments require that you use it, here are some tips for adjusting your combination to succeed one assignment at a time.

- Do not get upset about mistakes; think of them as steps to completing an assignment.
- Seek another person's opinion to strengthen your own opinions.
- When given an assignment, reflect on different ways of completing the assignment.

- Talk to others to get ideas you can shape into your own.
- Do not hesitate to start an assignment because of time or information; corrections can always be added later.
- Take small chances at new or creative ways of completing assignments until you feel comfortable taking greater risks.

## When *Your* Combination Is Not *My* Learning Combination

We as teachers have a great deal of work to do to encourage learners to accept, enjoy, and even relish their patterns—and most of all, use them to achieve success in learning. To be able and willing to do this requires considerable flexibility.

From the very first pages of this text, the question that all of this has been leading up to is quite simply, "Are you a part of the lehr-industrial model of teaching, or are you prepared to work with students to help them unlock their will to learn?" If you answer "yes" to lehr-model, then negotiating and strategizing with students concerning their learning combinations are not activities in which you are willing to engage. If, on the other hand, you are prepared to work with learners on the basis of the knowledge of how children learn interactively, then you are ready to develop the skills of facilitating students' unlocking of their will to learn. You will find the remainder of the book a resource guide for the development of your professional skills in this area.

## 13

*E pluribus unum*
—U.S. motto (inscription on the
Great Seal of the United States)

# Making Sense of Our Combinations

We began Part 3 by reading about the Learning Combination Inventory and establishing that the LCI is a part of a process for unlocking a student's will to learn. It is important to end this section with that same message. It is also vital to reiterate that the LCI is not just an instrument—it is the beginning of an interaction between the learner and the teacher. The nature and the quality of that interaction is predicated on the learner's and the teacher's understanding of the LCI as an inventory of student responses to specific questions, not a measure of the learner's intellectual prowess or a description of the learner's personal belief system. The LCI is a reflection of the learner's interactive learning patterns. Its purpose is to promote, first and foremost, an "Aha!" an "OK!" and a "Yes!" response from the learner.

More specifically, the LCI process is aimed at raising learners' awareness of their individual and highly internalized interactive learning systems. The "Aha!" response is the confirmation learners feel when the inventory confirms for them what they have already sensed or experienced about their learning methods. The LCI process also opens up for them an understanding and appreciation of the interactive learning system of others. That is the "OK!" or affirmation experience. It's the "It's OK to be different" affirmation; it's the "It's OK for others to be different from me" awareness. The LCI process encourages learners to use their learning patterns appropriately during the school day. That's the "Yes! I can." "Yes, I will apply what I know to this assignment. I'll negotiate some changes with the teacher." Or it's the "I need to look at my general strategies and apply them to get through this assignment without feeling unsuccessful. If I know how to apply myself, then I'm willing to put forth the effort that it takes to succeed."

The development of the learner's confirmation, affirmation, and application skills is central to the LCI process. It is the outcome that is sought. It places the learner front and center, and it does so in a most positive manner.

Now follows the word of caution. So often in our schooling experience, both as students and as teachers, we find ourselves comparing ourselves with others, comparing one student with another— more than that, we find ourselves comparing numbers, ascribing greater value to some than to others. We use these numbers, or in the case of instruments, we use the scores to evaluate, label, classify, divide, and separate. We ascribe an order of value and worth. We identify deficiencies, and we prescribe remediation. To do that with the outcomes of the LCI would be to violate the concept, the purpose, and the spirit of the process.

First of all, if the message has not been clearly stated before, it needs to be stated bluntly now: No one schema is better than another! No one learning schema is the pattern of a gifted student; no one schema is the pattern of a classified student; no one pattern is the schema of a successful student or the pattern of a failure. Schemas are not inherently good or bad; schemas don't have greater or lesser potential. The key is that those students who are successful as learners are those who have an understanding of their learning behaviors and know when and how to use them to their advantage; that is first and foremost. Second, these students appear to have the most external support, recognition, acceptance, encouragement, and, if desired, coaching to use their natural learning patterns to achieve inside and outside the classroom.

No one schema is better than another!

**No one schema is better than another!**

## Center Stage or Upstaged?

It is, I am certain, human nature to want to think that our human abilities or mental resources are exceptional. The Learning Combination Inventory cannot be used—should not be used—to promote that human foible. I have some information that may help put to rest any idea that one schema or one set of learning patterns is better than another. There are many ways to provide evidence of this, but I think one of the most fun is to play a game: Can You Tell the Difference? See how you score.

### Can You Tell the Difference?

*How universal are our learning schemas?*

Read the student statements recorded below. See if you can label each of the responses on the basis of the age, educational program, and geographic location of the respondent. Choose one descriptive category from each of the three main headings and place the letter or numeral next to each response:

| AGE | EDUCATIONAL PROGRAM | LOCALE |
|---|---|---|
| a = age 6-11 | I = regular education | 1 = East Coast, U.S.A. |
| b = age 12-22 | II = special education | 2 = South, U.S.A. |
| | III = Westinghouse National Science Scholar | 3 = Republic of Malta |
| | | 4 = Belfast, N. Ireland |

**What makes learning frustrating for me?**

_____ 1. "If I can't understand the directions."

_____ 2. "When the teacher doesn't give full directions, and I can't find a way to do the work."

_____ 3. "I don't work well when I don't have good instructions or the teacher doesn't do a good job of explaining the assignment."

_____ 4. "When I can't fully understand the directions and the teacher hasn't written them on the board."

**I would like the teacher to know how much I know . . .**

_____ 5. "By asking me some facts and questions. I like quizzes."

_____ 6. "By answering all the teacher's questions."

_____ 7. "By reading my work and asking me questions."

_____ 8. "By taking a test based on the detailed study guide the teacher gave."

**I would teach students by . . .**

_____ 9. "Having a better learning environment. How is learning fun when you are surrounded by 4 white cinder block walls with children's posters?"

_____ 10. "Taking more breaks and have lessons in the countryside."

_____ 11. "Exploring things around us. Our school is not a mile from a state park and yet we've never gone there to study anything, plants or animals."

_____ 12. "Doing more activities. Like we've got a miniature wood near us and we've never been in it. Instead of learning from drawings, we should go out to see things."

**I would like the teacher to know how much I know . . .**

_____ 13. "By taking tests—that way I know what I need to work on still without the embarrassment of being wrong in front of others."

_____ 14. "Taking notes and then 5 days later be asked questions to be sure I've been studying."

_____ 15. "Taking detailed notes and then doing activities to reinforce the information."

_____ 16. "Taking lots of notes and drawing out my opinion."

ANSWERS: 1. a-I-4; 2. b-I-2; 3. b-I-1; 4. b-II-1; 5. a-I-3; 6. b-I-1; 7. a-I-4; 8. b-I-2; 9. b-II-1; 10. b-I-3; 11. b-I-1; 12. a-I-4; 13. b-III-1; 14. b-I-3; 15. b-I-1; 16. a-I-4.

---

It should be obvious by now that it is impossible to determine the ethnic, geographic location, age, or educational program of these responses. Schemas appear to be quite universal.

The issue is not "How much better is one schema than another?" It is "How do I use my schema to unlock my will to learn, to strive, and to grow?" It would be interesting to study what intervening factors encouraged the students to strive—to overcome disabilities or use their schemas. I do have one insight to offer—the paragraph below written by a Westinghouse National Science Scholar:

> I am a person who sees the world through the eyes of a dyslexic. To compensate and adapt for this disability, occasionally I need extra time to complete assignments or tests, and a private area to read words aloud as necessary. I have been successful despite dyslexia because of my diligence and perseverance. [Learning combination: 34-29-27-24]

The point I am making is simply that no one schema is better or ensures more success for a student than another. What does make the difference is using the schema you have to achieve. I think the dyslexic scholar has used her schema to its highest potential. Even as she writes about her countless hours of hard work and her independent research, I see a learner who has come to grips with her learning processes and has gone the extra mile to unlock her will to learn.

I believe that such success is best enabled when the learner and the teacher have knowledge of and respect for the varieties of schemas that are found in the classroom. One of the most interesting things I have discovered is that the four patterns of interactive learning are found among persons young and old, rural and urban, and students in regular education, special education, and gifted education. All we need as learners and teachers is the commitment to unlock these combinations and the will to use them—that's all—and, frankly speaking, whether we like it or not, as educational leaders in the classroom, the use of the interactive learning model needs to begin with us!

Latin proverb: "The drop makes the hole in the stone not through its force but by constant falling." This is the effect of the persistent will to learn.

C. Voelker, personal correspondence, June 24, 1995[1]

## Note

1. Personal communication used with permission of Courtney Voelker.

# PART
# 4

# PUTTING OUR WILL TO WORK

## Before We Conclude

Part 4 brings us full circle. This text began by placing the learner center stage. It was inevitable that we come to this point—the point of "now what?" Now that I understand more about the learning process, what am I to do? Now that I know more about my learning pattern, what am I to do? Now that I recognize learners' patterns of learning, what am I to do? *Now, what?*

Part 4 provides some answers to these *what* questions, including how to engage our will to teach—more specifically, how to engage our will to teach to engage the student's will to learn. The chapters of Part 4 contain more practical approaches to using the LCI process. This is the challenging part for the teacher and learner. It is also the most fun.

Where there is no vision, the
people perish.
—Proverbs 29:18 (New
International Version)

# Where There
# Is No Vision

## Teaching Can Become So Daily

Recently, I heard a phrase used to describe the plight of teaching.
Its simple depth really struck me. "We teach so daily." I asked the
individual who had used this phrase to explain what she meant. She
said,

> We teach what we've grown comfortable with. Many of us,
> especially in this district, take time to learn about various
> trends in education, but we have so many other things to handle
> that we ultimately end up teaching in bits and pieces. Our goal
> becomes to get through the next class period—to get through
> the day—to get through the week. We do it day in and day out.
> We don't even realize we are doing it. It's like I said, "We teach
> so daily."

All teachers wrestle with this problem. Veteran teachers—good
teachers—wrestle with the "routineness" of teaching. After awhile,
you can tell the season of the year by the story you've done, the math
problems you are on at this time of the year, the civil war battle being
taught, the conjugation of the irregular verb, and so on and so on. In
fact, one of the most common reasons teachers give for not doing lesson
plans is that "I've taught this for so many years, I could do this

blindfolded—with my hands tied behind my back—in the dark." New teachers wrestle with the "daily-ness" of survival: "I managed this class, but how will I get through the next group?"

Unintentionally, teaching becomes so *daily;* unintentionally, teaching loses sight of the learner.

## Where There Is No Vision, Teaching Perishes

"Losing sight" is an important phrase to understand. Losing sight may occur because we no longer have clear vision—not eyesight, but a vision of our purpose as educators. Loss of vision results in a loss of the larger picture, a loss that occurs when we can no longer see beyond the papers to be graded, the stack of tests to be corrected, the number of progress reports to be filled out. It can also occur when we have lost sight of our sense of purpose. It happens when we lose our verve—our will to teach.

Without vision—without our "eye on the prize"—the will to teach is subverted into survival skills. As described in Part 1 of the text, we are inundated with the daily-ness of memos, paperwork, phone calls, discipline slips, and on and on. Where is the learner in all this? Where is the teacher? Where is our focus? Where is our energy—our motivation? What happens to our "bold reason" for being there, our badge of purpose? Without a vision, it is exhausted and misplaced. "Without vision" is true for teachers, also!

The best way to combat daily-ness is to have sound vision. Vision is a clear mental image of a preferable future. It fends off daily-ness by requiring us to base our action on continuous personal and professional growth. Vision instructs us and directs us. It gives meaning to our professional lives. Vision is value based. It does not allow us to fall victim to daily-ness. Vision is change oriented, not for the sake of change but for *our* sake. It removes fear and replaces it with reasoned risk. It guides, directs, and keeps us from pretending not to know—not to know what is best for the learner. Vision makes it possible for us to hold up the learner as central to schooling and to hold up our commitment to teaching as central to the learner. Vision is our conscience—our bead on learning. It is the touchstone, the centering mechanism. It lies at the center of our will to teach.

## Where There Is No Vision, the Learner Perishes

Learners are astute. They observe the daily-ness of teaching—the "Open your books to page _____," the "Get out your workbooks," the "Exchange papers and follow along while I read the answers," the "Do problems 1 to 15, every other one." They hear the subject matter being taught. They don't always understand how it relates to them. The learners in this situation lack the vision of what teaching, the classroom, and

Barna, 1992

Glickman, 1991

**Vision makes it possible for us to hold up the learner as central to schooling and to hold up our commitment to teaching as central to the learner.**

To be truly acquainted with a person means to be able to take his point of view, to think within his frame of reference, to reason from his premises.
—Allport, as quoted in Assagioli, 1973, p. 259

learning in this context is all about. As a result, they lose motivation—they lose their will to learn. Without vision, the learner also perishes.

> From my earliest memories of school, I can recall having an anxiety about sitting in a classroom with unfamiliar people and being forced to learn. I had always felt that the educational setting was more like a punishment or jail sentence than a safe harbor for learning. Students were sentenced during the first week of September and paroled during the third week of June. I hated school, but I didn't know why. Each day I would ask myself the same question, "Why am I here?"
>
> For one thing, I didn't enjoy sitting at my desk doing rows and rows of math problems. I've always enjoyed having a debate or problem solving. I think some of my frustration was created by the insecurity I felt when I just didn't want to be sitting in the classroom participating in activities that I had little interest in and felt little importance in completing.
>
> My favorite "class" was recess because that was unrestricted time where I could do what interested me with nobody telling me if my performance was adequate. Recess was a catharsis, it allowed me to release my classroom anxiety while recharging my energies to make it through the rest of the day.
>
> In terms of my learning, I am very analytical. Everything has to make sense. The majority of what I have learned, I have assessed and analyzed myself. In the majority of my classes, I would prefer to be in the corner by myself trying to figure something out without someone directing me or looking over me. Trial and error was and continues to be the most important component of my learning processes. Practical and analytical problem solving is the key for me.
>
> It took me a long time to understand how to be a successful student. I have figured out that the key to becoming a good student is to develop your own strategy or process for learning and use that process everyday. I know you can't set up a program for everybody dying in the classroom. But something has to be done.

What I have come to learn about how students learn is not all of them do.
—G. Dainton, personal communication, October 11, 1993

Johnston & Dainton, 1994b, pp. 61-63[1]

Daily-ness causes us to lose sight of the learner and to lose sight of who we are as teachers. How can we regain it—that sense of purpose, that sense of "I have an important reason to be here"? That sense of caring about the learner? That sense of professional commitment to teaching?

It is our duty as educators to protect a child's potential, not destroy it.
—Boyer, 1993

## Restoring the Vision

Restoring our vision—our will to teach—may be as uncomplicated as sitting down and reflecting on the key question: What do I see as the preferable future of my teaching? For example, my professional vision is, "All learners thrive here!" This is based on my belief that I am here to teach learners how to learn. Within my classroom environment, I will use my vision to develop a sense of mission, a set of goals, and a strategy for teaching that makes my vision a reality. My commitment is, "I am prepared to use my informed effort, my engaged effort, and my reflective effort to accomplish this." The subject matter is the vehicle I use to teach learners to learn. I teach them about themselves and about each other. I teach them to make decisions about their learning behaviors. I teach them how to thrive as learners within my subject matter and beyond. Every lesson plan I write, every act of discipline I do, every home contact is done from this perspective—with this vision in mind. It is all done with my sense of mission clearly in place and with my sense of who the student is as a learner and who I am as a teacher firmly in hand.

## Creating the Mission

**Mission is vision in action.**

Mission is vision in action. The statement of mission gives the broad-stroke vision grounding in the realities of the situation. The mission statement forms the basis for strategic planning. Here I am going to risk a reader's groan when I suggest that mission is the ultimate lesson plan—not the daily lesson plan written in a 3-by-3-inch square, but a profession-long plan for learner-teacher interaction. For the teacher who has grasped the vision of the will to teach, the mission becomes the personal platform—the verbalized, articulated substance of the will to teach. The mission statement/teacher platform spells out what the teacher believes gives meaning to teaching—meaning that provides centering to teaching energy, to the effort to help students unlock the will to learn.

In the previous paragraphs, I have shared my sense of vision and mission. Following next are not my words but the work of two teachers—one with less than 5 years of experience and one with more than 20. Read, digest, and reflect—see their vision, identify their sense of mission, and recognize the will to teach found in each personal teaching platform:

### Platform 1

To be a teacher you must be willing to walk a fine line between enlightenment and despair. If you can overcome the social stigma of "just being a teacher," you must then confront the true challenges of the vocation you have chosen. You must be willing to accept the phenomenal responsibility of the education of your future, while coping with the mundane and usually trivial complications of being a teacher operating in the monstrous bureaucratic machine of life. Anyone who does anything has learned from a teacher. We are all learners, just as we are all teachers. But some of us do the latter and get paid for it. I believe I could teach without ever receiving any monetary compensation, yet I accept my salary, seeing that as a reward for being able to teach in spite of the cynical world, the strangling rules, and the relentless bureaucracy in which a teacher does his job.

Educating a young person is not simply cramming her mind with as much objective knowledge as is deemed proper by administrators. A teacher must realize that he is involved with the development of a life. Furthermore, the teacher must understand that he is receiving a student who is certainly not a carte blanche; that student has been previously molded and has developed into a young person capable of making decisions and who already has a particular way of translating the world around her. In other words, for the teacher and student alike, there is never objective knowledge without subjective knowledge. Each student brings with them to the classroom their own cultural capital, making them individuals in every aspect, including how they learn.

A math teacher teaches math, a reading teacher teaches reading, and so on. Yet all teachers are teaching other values besides their specific discipline. Certainly, a math teacher and his students do not operate in a mathematical vacuum. The student should adequately learn the subject matter, but she also should learn how to abide by the social rules and expectations set up in the microcosm called the classroom, and she should learn to value learning for the sake of being a better person. All of what a student learns in a math class, including non-mathematical ideas, will be carried out of the classroom and eventually out of the school with that student as she becomes a viable citizen of the community. Since it is better to build a child than to repair an adult, a teacher must understand that every aspect of the time he is with a student affects the kind of person she will become.

Yet it is the authority of those who teach that is often a hindrance to those who learn. A problem exists when the teacher has dug a moat around himself and declared that, since he holds the answer key, he is the be-all and end-all. That teacher is not a leader of students, nor a facilitator of learning; his students are completely disempowered. A teacher must break down these barriers; he must turn over the learning to the students, so that they can truly have ownership of their education. A teacher must reduce the risk a student feels in learning while building the trust the student needs to succeed. Without being a monopolizer of information, a teacher must be a facilitator; without being a tyrant, a teacher must be firm; without being a friend, a teacher must be approachable. A teacher needs to establish a classroom that is a safe, fair, and conducive place for learning to take place.

Evans, 1995[2]

### Platform 2

My teaching platform is not expressed in the intellectual language of the scholars. It is a reflective statement of what I have lived and experienced during the past 21 years as teacher and now as an administrator. As a teacher/administrator in a large urban setting, I'm sure that my educational ideology may differ drastically from one who has had quite a contrasting experience.

First and foremost, education should be the primary tool to aid in the development of one reaching his or her true aspirations. A truly educated person is one who has gained an understanding of his or her environment and is able to use the resources available to enhance his or her life. The context in which many students experience the educational process prohibits them from growing into a productive adulthood.

A meaningful education is not played out by a given set of rules, monotonously patterned or programmed in black and white text. Education is the human resource of empowerment. It is the quality and relevance of the educational experience that will empower our youth to become independent thinkers and productive adults in a society that will demand the use of high-tech skills as we move toward the 21st century.

Teaching a child to read and write, for the most part, is a rote task accomplished again and again without much thought process. However, teaching that same child to seek, explore, gain, and then value an identity that expands imagination and expectations is the challenge we must face. An educator's real task is to help nurture the talents of young people so that they are able to overcome self-doubt, low expectations, and a lack of self-respect. A child must see himself or herself as the subject of the curriculum, not the object of teaching.

Whether reading, writing, or tapping into Internet, my role as an educator is to make certain that students are engaged in a meaningful process. I must provide opportunities for them to respond, react and then relate to an experience instead of possibly leading them to engage in using lower-level thinking skills, which frequently results in extreme apathetic behavior.

There is no doubt that many major environmental factors such as economics, the drug culture, and loss of morality and values have taken a toll on the urban education scene. In addition, the frustration of focusing on the basic skills has also been the demise of many of our children in the classroom. The "state" blinds our vision until we see no other recourse but to drill, drill, and drill! Over a period of time, the monotony and irrelevance of the curriculum smothers all creative and reflective thinking and thus destroys one's identity and level of self-worth. This cycle must be broken if students are to employ the use of analysis, synthesis and evaluation in their quest for knowledge.

Not only will urban education benefit, but the entire educational arena will if we reassess the procedures and methods of teaching our children. As administrators and teachers, we are faced with an urgent challenge. Through our direction and teaching, let's empower kids with confidence, high expectations, and self-respect. Then and only then can we truly say that we have helped to shape the lives of productive adults.

Brown, 1995[3]

## Developing the Vision: Myopic or Hyperopic

I had a professor friend who used to charge out of his office before each class and announce, "I'm off to do battle with ignorance—to hold back its threat from the borders of my students' minds." I thought, "Well, good for you. I'm off to meet 27 graduate students who paid their tuition and expect a darn good show." These statements represent two extremes of vision: hyperopic—the grand vision—and myopic—the cryptic shortsightedness of a harried teacher. Neither of these represents the vision of which I am speaking.

For further reading, see Palonsky (1986).

## Perish the Thought

The development of a professional vision and mission as a teacher is a process. It is essential to participating in the Learning Combination Inventory process—without it, the use of the LCI will not come to fruition.

It is logical to assume that if the information you have gained about the Interactive Learning Model is accurate, then you will choose to use your newly informed effort to engage in reflection—healthy, positive reflection—about your teaching, a reflection that causes you to ask, "How can I make what I have learned within these pages a reality in my classroom?" This is the challenge facing each teacher who is committed to putting the learner center stage. If we do not address this matter within the pages of this text, readers can keep all that they read up to this point quite cerebral and quite safe—locked away. But this book is about unlocking learning, so I emphasize that if you intend to implement what you have read—to put into practice the insights you've gained about student-learners and teacher-learners, then you will seek to develop your sense of vision and mission as a self-renewing process that engages *your* will to learn in the will to teach!

I've come to the frightening conclusion that I am the decisive element in the classroom. It's my personal approach that creates the climate. It's my daily mood that makes the weather.

As a teacher, I possess a tremendous power to make a child's life miserable or joyous. (Ginott, 1972, p. 15)

## Notes

1. Used by permission.
2. Unpublished teaching platform used by permission of John Evans.
3. Unpublished teaching platform used by permission of Brenda K. Brown.

# 15

What would happen if we treated the student as someone whose opinion mattered?
—Fullan, 1991, p. 170

# Not a Rock in the Bag; a Tool in the Kit (for Teacher and Learner Alike)

## Not a Rock, a Tool

Some time ago, the superintendent of one of the districts in which I was piloting the Learning Combination Inventory commented to me, "The thing I like about this approach to learning is it does not become another rock in the teacher's bag; it's a tool in the teacher's kit." His comment made me smile as I resonated to this metaphorical depiction of the process. I think that accurately describes the LCI process and the message I am seeking to convey throughout this book.

J. Graves, personal communication, November 4, 1994

## Rocks Are Burdens; Tools Are Remedies

The rock-tool metaphor has stuck with me probably because I carry a tapestry shoulder bag wherever I go. There are those who tease me about my "feed bag," but that catchall bag is much more "me" than a briefcase. If you were to pick it up and inspect its contents, you would find that I carry no rocks in that bag; I carry the professional tools of my trade. I do not view the items found within the bag—the notebooks, journals, date books, Kappan *Fastbacks,* the research articles, the note cards, idea banks, student papers, student portfolios, alternative assessment projects, data disks, and so forth—burdensome. I see them as the work-products of my students' learning schemas—the work-product of my tools for teaching, my chosen responsibility, and my professional opportunity. And yes, I use the LCI with my students, and I work to teach them how to learn more about their learning schemas.

Even at the graduate level, I hold to the belief that the responsibility of learning is the learner's; the responsibility for teaching the learner how to learn is the teacher's. Teaching a learner to learn is not a burden for the teacher to bear. Teaching a learner to learn is an opportunity to assist the learner in unlocking the will to learn. I have not abandoned what I know about learning simply because the age of the typical teacher-learner with whom I work lies between 25 and 60!

I have learned from using the LCI process that it takes time; it takes patience; it challenges me to do things differently from when I began graduate-level instruction. But when all is said and done, the work of learning has shifted to its rightful owner—the student—and the work of teaching the learner how to learn has evolved into a much more defined responsibility for me as a professor.

Does this happen overnight? No. Does it happen incrementally? Yes. Does it require hours and hours of testing and conferencing? No, not if the teacher and the learner recognize that the LCI process is a continuing process—a series of dialogues and exchanges, a set of conversations that occur within specific learning contexts and assignments. Remember, the LCI process is a commitment to communicate, to dialogue, to work together as learner and teacher throughout the length of the learning experience.

## How to Get Beyond the Rock Sensation

Instead of talking all the time about what teachers should teach and what students should learn, we should talk about what teachers and students should do. We should be talking about experiences they should be mutually engaged in.
—Smith, 1995, p. 590

The LCI process does not add to your already-full bag of "what a teacher should do." In fact, when used properly, the LCI process provides you with a means of removing some of the burdensome rocks that you have been carrying around with you for some time—rocks such as "What a student learns depends on me." "How well a student-learner does on a standardized test rests on my shoulders." "If I don't teach that fact, that spelling rule, that play, that theory, that formula, that . . ., that . . ., that . . ., the student won't know," which translates into "the student hasn't learned," which translates into "and it's all my fault." The rocks get heavier and heavier with each item added to a curriculum, with each state-mandated subject, and with each local policy decision.

When you recognize that the work of learning is not yours and that the work of learning is the student's, then the question shifts to "How can I equip the student to learn?" Here is where the teacher has the opportunity and responsibility to do the teaching.

## Why Make the Shift From Rock to Tool

The shift from teaching subject matter to teaching learners is not new to teaching. Interestingly, it has been around for a long time. It is a grossly underused awareness:

> The task of the teacher is to stir-up connections between the pupil's (learning) nature and the subject whether in line of theoretic curiosity, of personal interest, or pugnacious impulse. The laws of the mind will then bring enough pulses of effort into play to keep the pupil exercised in the direction of learning. (James, 1904, p. 83)

> Children lose when they restrict themselves to "what was taught" and ignore learning about their own natural abilities and knowledge. (Caine & Caine, 1991, p. 123)

> Your job is not to fill empty heads with facts for the present but, more important, to excite children about learning for the many years to come, in and out of school. (Yellin & Blake, 1994, p. 4)

If you believe teaching is learner centered, if you believe that unlocking a student's will to learn is vital, if you believe that developing your will to teach is paramount, then you will be willing to invest the time to implement the LCI process. And it is an investment, not only of time but of yourself, in the learner. It cannot be explained as anything less than that. It is time well spent, however. It does not create another rock in your bag—it is a tool in your kit. You need to view it and use it as such.

## Sharing the Tool Kit: Teaching Ourselves Out of a Job

The concern over rocks and tools may actually be a matter of who has control. The basis of this text is that the learner controls the learning; the teacher controls the teaching. The issue is what you want

Redding, 1990

to contribute to the classroom and how you want to make that contribution. If the learner controls learning, then doesn't it make sense to equip the learner to do the learning rather than attempting to do the learning for the learner? We have for too long attempted (unsuccessfully, I might add) to do the work of learning *for* our students. The work of learning is the student's. Redding is right: The primary cause of learning is the activity of the learner's own mind. Why, then, do we devote our teaching energies to putting information into the heads of our students? Why not equip them to do the work—teach them about learning—teach them about themselves and how to unlock their learning skills—teach them to understand their own learning processes and to use them appropriately? Why not do this? As one teacher put it, "But if we do that, we would be teaching ourselves right out of a job." That would not be a reason to mourn; that would be a reason to rejoice!

The message of this book is "Let's get on with letting the student learn. The sooner we become participant-observers in the learning process, the better!" There is good reason to take this approach. Much of the latest information about the motivational processes that affect student learning indicates clearly that students' failure to learn most

Dweck, 1986

frequently can be attributed to *lack of effort or lack of appropriate strategies for accomplishing the learning,* rather than ability. When students learn how to use their abilities and skills, they will persist and

Zimmerman & Martinez-Pons, 1988

persevere much longer at a learning task and will, therefore, achieve more than if they are only given feedback on their success or failure on a specific task.

## Tools for Rocks: The Necessity of Strategies for Learning

Learning how to use learning schemas is key to a student's overall success in learning—beginning with assuming responsibility for doing the work. That is why we need to be about "teaching students to do

Santrouck, 1994, p. 243

their job better." Remember, earlier, we discussed Santrouck's message: "Schooling will succeed . . . when children are encouraged to construct their own . . . knowledge." We now know the deeper meaning of that statement.

We understand the interactive processes that learners use to construct knowledge. We have the research basis that tells us that within given subject areas, teaching specific techniques or strategies for using sequence, precision, technical reasoning, and unique solutions *do* make a difference in students' ability to learn the subject matter. We also

Winne & Marx, 1980

Peterson, 1982

know the importance of understanding learners' *natural strategies* for learning to teach a *new strategy* to the learners. We know that the simple observation of students is not sufficient to give the teacher an accurate picture of how "instruction" is actually being received and digested by the learners. Finally, we have solid evidence that using specific strategies has also proven to be much more effective than using global "study skills" to teach subject matter.

A large school district in Colorado has applied this knowledge with great success. Instead of simply "in-servicing" teachers on the importance of various theories-into-practice such as writing across the curriculum, whole language, the Hunter Model, Teacher Effectiveness Student Achievement, alternative assessment, and cooperative learning, the district has had the teachers teach the students about these processes—why they have chosen to use them, what they expect of learners as a result of it, and so forth. They have experienced amazing success. Obviously, they have decided to place the tools of learning into the hands of the students. Their approach has been as follows:

- Teach students what enhances and what impedes learning.
- Help students recognize and develop their learning strengths.
- Teach specific learning strategies.
- Pass on the responsibility of learning to the student.

We can equip learners with the tools to thrive within the school setting. The teaching activities described above are living proof of the doability of placing learners center stage and providing learners with an awareness of their interactive learning systems. The process should begin with a declaration by the teacher to the learners that from the first day until the final day of the school year, you, the teacher, are investing in the learners' learning. You may want to post your vision on the board: **All Learners Thrive Here!**

Here is the learner. This is why we have school—for the sake of the learner. So, if we don't understand the learner, then we are not going to be able to address the real purpose of school—the development of the learner. If we do not understand the learner as a whole person, then we are contributing to the learner's being less than she or he can be. As we understand the learner, we can help the learner to understand him- or herself. This enables the learner to gain from schooling—the educational process needed to become a mature learner.

Now is our opportunity to begin thinking about how to encourage and teach our student-learners to represent their own knowledge. I am certain that we, at first, will struggle alongside the learners with the issue of how to do this. But if we are serious about understanding learners, and if we are serious about helping learners understand themselves, then this is an opportunity—an opportunity, not a burden—an opportunity as a "locksmith" to help learners unlock the will to learn.

The idea of student responsibility for learning does not imply a lessened teacher responsibility for teaching. [It implies teaching about] strategies for learning and achievement.
—Wittrock, 1994, p. 306

Redding, 1990

Becoming aware of one's own strengths and weaknesses leads to more personal responsibility for choices in the learning situation and thus more self-regulation.
—Schmeck, 1988, pp. 344-345

Only those forms of motivational orientation that are directed at the act of learning itself facilitate positive learning experiences.
—Schiefele & Csikszentmihalyi, 1994, p. 265

I am a professional, and I will continue to act and think like one. I will empower children by helping them learn how to learn "that all children may learn."
—Blowe, journal entry, June 5, 1995

Teachers need to think about how students think, listen to them describe what helps them learn, and create with their colleagues activities and methods that get closer to active learning [in the manner in which the students describe they learn].
—Glickman, 1991, p. 6

The idea is to have you understand the learner as a learner—to have you help each learner understand him- or herself—to transform the "rock" sensation in your teaching bag into a tool in the learner's kit.

As learners and teachers, we are complex—but we are understandable. If we take the time to learn about ourselves as learners and then take the same time to listen to students—to help them understand their learning schemas, our students will have a great deal more respect for us as caregivers and educators. If we approach them in this honest manner, and if we approach them by saying, "This is how I learn, and it may not be how you learn, but let's work it out together," then we have freed ourselves of the burdensome rocks of schooling and have taken up the tools of authentic learning.

# 16

Students are entitled to an education that is suitable to them.
—Postman, 1979, p. 228

# Nothing Ventured, Nothing Gained

## Make and Take

As a secondary school teacher, I always envied elementary teachers who went to workshops and returned to school with all sorts of ideas and projects to use in the classroom. These "make-and-take" activities are a great way to bring theory and practice together. Now, in this final chapter, I have an opportunity to conduct my own make-and-take workshop. Of course, I realize that although I can make these suggestions, it is up to you, the reader, to "take" them or leave them. Some of these ideas will "fit," and others won't, depending on your interactive learning process and dominant schema. Each idea is offered with the hope that it will contribute to making education more suitable to the learners in your classroom.

## Make a Beginning

If you are wondering how to begin using the LCI process in your classroom, I suggest the following steps. Determine which are workable for you and your learners.

**Step 1:** During the first week of school, administer the appropriate level of the Learning Combination Inventory to your students. As much as possible, have the students participate in filling out the scoring sheets and completing the bar graphs.

**Step 2:** Be certain to clarify the accuracy of the "combination" of learning schemas.

**Step 3:** Begin your one-on-one or small-group discussion of what the learning combination means.

**Step 4:** Consider having the younger students make a "lock" manipulative to keep as a handy reminder for discussing and explaining their combinations (see Appendix B).

**Step 5:** Consider having the older students develop a succinct, one-sentence learner vision statement and/or an expanded mission statement that could be presented orally, in writing, pictorially, musically, and so forth. Remember, in each instance, to allow learners the time and space to develop a response that demonstrates their schemas. You don't want to defeat the purpose of this activity! You will need clear directions, some examples, and an open mind that permits a variety of optional responses.

**Step 6:** Take time during the first week to have students pair up or "group up" and visit with others in class whose LCIs are similar. Have an interview format available for those learners who would like guidance in doing the activity. Emphasize that this is an opportunity to find a "learn-alike" in the classroom—a soul mate of sorts. Some students will delight in this. Others might hold back and listen. Don't be concerned.

**Step 7:** It is vital that you also take time to have students pair up or group up with others in class whose LCIs are not similar. Have an interview format available for those who would like structure to getting to know more about how others approach learning. Again, some students might hold very brief conversations. Don't be concerned by this.

An excellent culminating activity is to engage the learners in a cooperative learning project. You may begin it by telling the learners that you are intentionally putting them into learning groups on the basis of a balance of their LCIs. That means you will have balanced the group's composition of dominant "I use this first" schemas and "I avoid this" schemas.

Then give each group a subject-relevant learning task that requires the deliberate use of all four schemas. Have materials and various drafting, drawing, or other "gadgets" available to each group. Earlier in the text, I mentioned the example of the family shield, but there are other "first of the year" activities that are less involved. For example, you may ask the students to develop an object, a program, or an activity that they would like to see become a regular part of the classroom for the year.

The students are to plan their approach, write a summary of what they would do, demonstrate how their project would work, and give it a unique title or label. Remember, do not permit the students to set off on this learning adventure without talking to them about how to avoid their old routines of competition and isolation. In lieu of that behavior and in light of what they have learned about each other during the previous week's orientation to the LCI process, encourage the groups to begin their work by identifying the different learning schemas within their group. Model how to do this before you turn the groups loose to begin their work.

Depending on the sophistication and age of the students, you may want to allow an entire class period for this activity. Once the task is complete, have the students remain in their groups and give feedback to each other, concentrating on how they did the task and what they observed about how each member contributed to the outcome. Here's a list of behaviors to use when "I.D.-ing" the participants:

- Who insisted on following the directions and suggested developing a plan before you began? Who arranged the task items or materials neatly? Who cleaned up without being told to?

- Who kept asking specific questions or kept referring to the book looking for more information? Who kept the notes? Who explained the project or took time to write down what to say for the explanation of the group's work-product? Who spoke up without being asked and gave the most detailed explanation of what was done by the group?

- Who offered the least verbal explanation while remaining on-task, fascinated by the mechanical or technical items used to complete the assignment? Who appeared to prefer to work alone or to take charge and handle the task by him- or herself? Who played with the gadgets? Who built the actual end product?

- Who generated the most ideas? Who kept wanting to start over? Who wanted to ignore the directions and proceed in a "different" manner? Who kept interrupting the work with "just one more idea" right up until the completion of the task?

Discuss what worked, what didn't, and how well the learners communicated with each other during the task. Do not be afraid to discuss who or what got on whose nerves, where extreme patience was required and exercised, and so on. This may require some carryover time from the day of the task to the beginning of the next class period. Doing this activity in this manner, however, is very important.

Making the effort and taking the time to do this at the beginning of the school year can result in your students' feeling that they are a part of a real learning community. No need to rush it or impose it. Let it build and grow under your guidance. Here are some additional make-and-take ideas.

## Makes and Takes

| | |
|---|---|
| *Make* your vision about teaching and learning known. | *Take* time to plaster your room with your vision and mission. |
| *Make* space in your orientation week to have students write their vision for learning in your classroom. | *Take* the three questions from the LCI as your prompts for helping students focus on their vision. ("If I were the teacher, I would have students learn by . . ." is a good place to begin.) |
| *Make* it clear that you are interested in helping. | *Take* time to discuss ways of assessing student work. ("How would you prefer to show your teacher what you have learned?") |
| *Make* every effort to discuss interactive learning patterns one-on-one and in small groups. | *Take* time to discover and to develop subject-relevant learning strategies. |
| *Make* time to allow your students to vent their frustration, evaluate their progress, collaborate with fellow learners, and celebrate small victories. | *Take* time for yourself to vent your frustration, evaluate your progress, talk with your students, collaborate with fellow teachers, and celebrate small victories. |

**Box 16.1.**

These activities or ones similar to those in the previous section, "Making a Beginning," not only help to form the basis of a real learning community in which the learner is center stage but also help to establish a learning community that operates with very cooperative, cooperative learning!

## Take It or Make It Better: Cooperative Learning

Cooperative learning is usually defined as students working together in groups with group goals but individual accountability. When implemented well, cooperative learning produces increased student achievement and positive learning behaviors. For those reasons, cooperative learning appeals to teachers who "hunger for ways to work with

McFarland, 1992, p. 2

kids in heterogeneous groups and be more successful at it." To achieve these learning goals, however, it is essential when forming cooperative learning groups to "place students wisely!"

Ellis & Whalen, 1992, p. 35

What does wise placement look and sound like? During the past 3 years, I have studied cooperative learning strategies in a number of districts and at various grade levels. The random assignment versus intentional placement of students on the basis of their interactive learning schemas has made a significant difference in how students view cooperative learning as a group technique as well as how they view their fellow classmates. Learners who were placed in cooperative learning groups on the basis of their interactive learning patterns had a good sense of what they could contribute to the group. The opening words of an interview I completed with Mae, a student whose placement was on this basis, begins with

> How long will this interview take? My group needs me. I take the notes and keep track of what we agree to do. If I'm not there, no one else does it. They depend on me, so I can't be gone too long.

I was impressed by the urgency in this young woman's voice as well as her ability to articulate her specific task and role within her group. On several occasions, two other observers and I had noted that this seventh grader demonstrated strong record-keeping skills and was able to use them within her group of highly charged young men who spent their time generating ideas and writing dialogue. I repeat, "Place students wisely."

The following anecdote tells the downside of cooperative learning when we do not heed the suggestion to "place students wisely."

> Eric looked defeated. The assignment was not complete. He had written only one line, and it didn't make much sense. His groupmates refused to sign the "letter" because they said "It's stupid." According to the assignment, what Eric had to turn in on behalf of the group was an incomplete product. Forty minutes before, the students had been given a set of directions by which to complete a math task. The explanation stated that the students were to read the information about the cost and habits of each fish. Next, they were to decide which fish they could afford to purchase that (a) would not fight with or harm other fish, (b) would not be too large for the hypothetical aquarium, and (c) would not exceed the amount budgeted. Finally, the students were to compose a letter to their teacher stating their decision and rationale. The letter was to be signed by all participants.

However, Jennifer was missing from their cooperative learning group that day. As described by her group members, Jennifer provided structure: "She always organizes us and writes down what we come up with. It always looks good and we get a good grade." But today, Jennifer was absent, and the rest of the cooperative learning team had assigned Eric to be recorder. Jack and TJ began working on the assignment. They calculated the cost of the fish and then turned the information over to Eric to put in its final form as per the directions for the cooperative learning exercise. Eric, who avoids precise processing and prefers technical reasoning, did the best he could. The product, however, included only one partial sentence and the picture of two fish drawn on the back of the "letter."

After the class left, I asked Eric what had happened. He said, "They're all angry with me because I didn't get the letter written." I asked, "What are the pictures for?" "Oh, those are the fish. See, they will fit in the aquarium. They are two types that won't fight. And see how much they cost. We spent as much money as we could without going over."

I looked at the $8\frac{1}{2} \times 11$ lined page. I didn't see any of Eric's explanation. All I saw were two small fish. Eric's explanation remained in his head. His classmates' signatures were not on the paper. The project had not been pulled off, and the group's perception of Eric's contribution was negative, as demonstrated by their lack of support for Eric's efforts, their refusal to sign the letter, and their comment, "This is really stupid." Eric was now the only student left in the classroom. He had put his head down on the desk and didn't appear ready to join the bustling hallway filled with his classmates.

Johnston & Dainton, 1994a, p. 11[1]

Mae and Eric are not isolated instances. Listen to still other voices of students who, within the context of our experiments, were placed in cooperative learning groups on the basis of random assignment:

— Nobody listens to me.
— I hate this group.
— I don't like this group. I got left doing everything.
— I'm concerned that we won't do well even though it sounds good to us.
— I wish I could send the two girls in our group to the moon and have them never come back.

Now listen to the voices of students who were placed in cooperative learning groups on the basis of a balance of their interactive learning schemas:

— I liked having others recognize what I could do for the group.
— I felt like they listened to me and depended on me for what I could do.
— I love to write things down, and that's what I do best. My group depends on me to make things look good when they are turned in.
— I discovered there is more than one way to solve a problem.

Johnston & Dainton, 1994a, p. 10

Any doubt about the importance of placing learners wisely? If you are interested in enhancing learning outcomes and building a learning community within your classroom, you will want to use the LCI process to assist you in formulating the groups. But remember, begin by completing the preliminary steps (see Steps 1 through 7) explained earlier in this chapter. When you do this, you will recognize the positive difference between intentional placement and random assignment. The words of Slavin ring true, and we need to heed them, especially when using cooperative learning activities: "Self-esteem occurs when students are each given special information that makes them indispensable to their groups." From our perspective, the special information that makes learners "indispensable to their group" is their learning schemas. It is this special information that once again places the learners center stage and allows the learners to shine!

Slavin, 1980, p. 339

## Make-or-Take Learning Activity Options

Up to this point in the chapter, I have consciously chosen to use a sequential format, one that allows both technical and confluent processors to have concise summaries of practical applications and imaginative kernels around which to develop the use of the LCI process within their classrooms. What follows are several precise examples you can use to reinforce your explanation of the learning schemas, have the learner identify with others of the same pattern, and develop a deeper understanding of the Interactive Learning Model and its application to many different experiences in life. You could also use these activities to maintain the LCI process as an important part of your classroom learning environment:

### *Manipulatives*

Build or construct the Learning Combination Lock Manipulative (see Appendix B). This is a series of concentric circles showing parts of the Interactive Learning Combination. When cut out and fastened at the center, the circles can be rotated to demonstrate a student's learning combination.

### *Current Event*

Clip current news articles that describe heroic, historical, or interesting characters. Bring them to class and discuss the schemas that these individuals have demonstrated by their words or actions. Use these examples to affirm the learners in your class.

The following is an example of a current event. An American pilot who escaped capture after his plane went down behind enemy lines was described in a syndicated news article. Note the words and phrases that suggest this individual's learning schema:

Cannon & Greve, 1995, p. 16

> "He was one of these people who put 100 percent into anything he did," recalled Eurana Wood, his sixth grade homeroom teacher. "He was so focused on whatever he did. Any project or task he finished thoroughly. It meant a lot to him to achieve or accomplish anything. He liked to chew on problem-solving things." His former football coach said, "He wasn't a quitter." A fellow pilot added, "He was no couch potato. He had a lot of experience in the woods and I think that helped him a lot."

## Sports Figure

Here is an example of a sports figure who describes his experiences in school. Note also his brother's description of his learning schema:

Gammons, 1990, p. 84

> "I have two brothers who got nothing but A's in school. I created the family curve. In high school I spent all my time on the baseball field and in the machine shop—working on motorcycles. I'm not smart." His brother Larry is quick to come to his defense. "We grew up with an engineering mindset because of my father. We're all analytical in our own way. Robin [Yount] looks at things and figures out why they work. When he was twelve, he took apart a motorcycle without anyone telling him how. On the golf course he'd study a putt for five hours if he had to. He would be one of the world's greatest teachers because he sees why things work and can explain them so kids understand."

## Fable

Use fables and have the children identify the schemas of the various characters. For example, you could use something as simple as "The Boy Who Cried Wolf." After discussing the little boy and what his possible schemas were, discuss what he would be like as a predominantly sequential processor, precise processor, and so forth. Have the students create a dialogue between the townspeople and the boy. Some may want to act this out.

## Literature

Use examples from classical or contemporary literature—novels, plays, biographies, and so forth.

### Historic Figures

Use historic figures such as presidents as examples of the various schemas: Herbert Hoover, sequential processor and organizer of food relief in Europe after World War II; Jimmy Carter, precise processor and nuclear engineer; Thomas Jefferson, technical processor, architect, and inventor; and Teddy Roosevelt, confluent processor and technical reasoner who relished the challenge of the outdoors and created his own approach to spelling.

### Contemporary Media

Use television characters from current shows with older students. Discuss their schemas. Discuss whether the character is stereotyped or displays an authentic interactive approach to learning.

Use figures (animated and real-life) from current movies, videos, and television to provide examples of schemas to which younger students might more readily relate.

Developing an awareness and use of interactive learning schemas requires practice through time. I have included these specific examples to illustrate how casually the schemas can be reinforced within the context of virtually every subject area on any given day. The LCI process can be continuing and deliberate without being "stand-alone" or topic fixated. How you choose to bring this information to the learner is your call. No list of six or seven approaches could come close to covering all the various means you have for accomplishing this. However you choose to reinforce the LCI process, make the most of the opportunities that arise during instructional activities. Each reinforcing activity will help your students learn about and appreciate themselves and their classmates as learners and as unique individuals. After all, isn't that what the learning process is all about?

## One Last Turn of the Dial;
## One Last Click of the Tumblers

You know and I know that these are the final pages of the book. As I write them, I feel that same sense of urgency that I do during the final class of the semester or the final class period of the school year. I must have more time to convey my message—one more opportunity for us to consider some great insight—one more chance to make a difference.

I vividly remember one of my 10th graders saying to me on the second to the last day of school, "Mrs. J., everybody else I know turned their textbooks in 2 weeks ago. Are we really going to be working up to the last day?" I was shocked. "What a foolish question," I thought.

"Of course we will be working. There is so much yet to do." Apparently, time and age have not mellowed that part of my will to teach because recently, at the conclusion of 5 grueling weeks of 4½ hours of course work per evening, I had suggested to the student-members of my five simulated school districts that we spend the last class session discussing learning outcomes and sharing portfolio contents. At that point, one of my more risk-taking students turned to me and said, "Doc, give it a rest. We have thought, talked, written, and done all there is to do. It's over." Though I forced a smile and appeared to quietly concede the point, I knew inside me *it* wasn't over. I was certain *it* wasn't over for those learners either—*it* was just beginning. I feel that same way about this text.

Although we have come to the final page of the text, I trust that this is not the end of your learning adventure. It is my belief—certainly my hope—that these pages mark the beginning of an even greater commitment on your part to invest personal and professional energies in your will to teach so that ultimately, those whom you serve are equipped to unlock their will to learn.

## Note

1. This and subsequent excerpts from Johnston and Dainton (1994a) are used with permission.

> *Our individual learning process is like a lock*
> *whose tumblers consist of*
> *how we know, how we take action, and what we feel.*
> *When patiently aligned and carefully executed,*
> *these tumblers open the vault wherein lies our will.*
>
> *The challenge we face as teachers and students*
> *is to identify the combination*
> *that unlocks our will to achieve any learning goal.*
> *—Johnston, 1993*

# Learning Combination Inventory

## "Unlocking the Will to Learn"

Form II

Your teachers and parents have probably told you many times that learning is an important part of life. Something they may not have told you is that we all learn in different ways. Each one of us has his or her own special learning combination. It is this combination which helps us think and understand, work and perform, develop and mature as capable, successful persons.

Your thoughtful responses to the following statements can help your teacher and you understand what your learning combination is. Please read each sentence carefully and respond to it as accurately as you can. If you have a question while completing this inventory, please ask your teacher to help you.

Name_____ Teacher_____

### Part I.

**Reminder:** This is not a test. It is a way to find out about how you accomplish learning tasks. Below are 28 statements each followed by five phrases that indicate how the statement might relate to you–"never ever," "almost never," "sometimes," "almost always," and "always." These phrases are numbered from one to five.

**Directions:** Here is what you are to do. 1) Read each sentence carefully. 2) Decide how well it fits what you do to learn. 3) Circle the numbered phrase that matches your response. 4) Write the number you have circled on the line to the left of the statement. 5) Be sure that you circle only one phrase for each statement.

**Let's practice!**

**Sample Statements:**

_____ A. I listen carefully when the teacher is giving directions.

| 1 | 2 | 3 | 4 | 5 |
|---|---|---|---|---|
| NEVER EVER | ALMOST NEVER | SOME-TIMES | ALMOST ALWAYS | ALWAYS |

_____ B. I like to stand in the front of the class and act out skits or plays.

| 1 | 2 | 3 | 4 | 5 |
|---|---|---|---|---|
| NEVER EVER | ALMOST NEVER | SOME-TIMES | ALMOST ALWAYS | ALWAYS |

**Words of Encouragement:** Remember, this is **not** a test! So, take all the time you need, and do the very best you can. Have fun, relax, and enjoy learning more about yourself.

_____ 1. I would rather build a project than read or write about a subject.

| 1 | 2 | 3 | 4 | 5 |
|---|---|---|---|---|
| NEVER EVER | ALMOST NEVER | SOME-TIMES | ALMOST ALWAYS | ALWAYS |

_____ 2. I need clear directions that tell me what the teacher expects before I begin an assignment.

| 1 | 2 | 3 | 4 | 5 |
|---|---|---|---|---|
| NEVER EVER | ALMOST NEVER | SOME-TIMES | ALMOST ALWAYS | ALWAYS |

_____ 3. I just enjoy generating lots of unique or creative ideas.

| 1 | 2 | 3 | 4 | 5 |
|---|---|---|---|---|
| NEVER EVER | ALMOST NEVER | SOME-TIMES | ALMOST ALWAYS | ALWAYS |

_____ 4. I memorize lots of facts and details when I study for a test.

| 1 | 2 | 3 | 4 | 5 |
|---|---|---|---|---|
| NEVER EVER | ALMOST NEVER | SOME-TIMES | ALMOST ALWAYS | ALWAYS |

_____ 5. I feel better about an assignment when I double-check my answers.

| 1 | 2 | 3 | 4 | 5 |
|---|---|---|---|---|
| NEVER EVER | ALMOST NEVER | SOME-TIMES | ALMOST ALWAYS | ALWAYS |

_____ 6. I like to take things apart to see how they work.

| 1 | 2 | 3 | 4 | 5 |
|---|---|---|---|---|
| NEVER EVER | ALMOST NEVER | SOME-TIMES | ALMOST ALWAYS | ALWAYS |

_____ 7. I am interested in knowing detailed information about whatever I am studying.

| 1 | 2 | 3 | 4 | 5 |
|---|---|---|---|---|
| NEVER EVER | ALMOST NEVER | SOME-TIMES | ALMOST ALWAYS | ALWAYS |

_____ 8. I like to come up with a totally new and different way of doing an assignment instead of doing it the same way as everybody else.

| 1 | 2 | 3 | 4 | 5 |
|---|---|---|---|---|
| NEVER EVER | ALMOST NEVER | SOME-TIMES | ALMOST ALWAYS | ALWAYS |

_____ 9. I prefer to take a paper and pencil test to show what I know.

| 1 | 2 | 3 | 4 | 5 |
|---|---|---|---|---|
| NEVER EVER | ALMOST NEVER | SOME-TIMES | ALMOST ALWAYS | ALWAYS |

_____ 10. I keep a neat notebook, desk, or work area.

| 1 | 2 | 3 | 4 | 5 |
|---|---|---|---|---|
| NEVER EVER | ALMOST NEVER | SOME-TIMES | ALMOST ALWAYS | ALWAYS |

_____ 11. I like to work with hand tools, power tools, and gadgets.

| 1 | 2 | 3 | 4 | 5 |
|---|---|---|---|---|
| NEVER EVER | ALMOST NEVER | SOME-TIMES | ALMOST ALWAYS | ALWAYS |

_____ 12. I am willing to risk offering new ideas even in the face of discouragement.

| 1 | 2 | 3 | 4 | 5 |
|---|---|---|---|---|
| NEVER EVER | ALMOST NEVER | SOME-TIMES | ALMOST ALWAYS | ALWAYS |

_____ 13. I need to have a complete understanding of the directions before I feel comfortable doing an assignment.

| 1 | 2 | 3 | 4 | 5 |
|---|---|---|---|---|
| NEVER EVER | ALMOST NEVER | SOME-TIMES | ALMOST ALWAYS | ALWAYS |

_____ 14. I find that researching information is my favorite way to learn a subject.

| 1 | 2 | 3 | 4 | 5 |
|---|---|---|---|---|
| NEVER EVER | ALMOST NEVER | SOME-TIMES | ALMOST ALWAYS | ALWAYS |

_____ 15. I like hands-on assignments where I get to use mechanical/technical instruments.

| 1 | 2 | 3 | 4 | 5 |
|---|---|---|---|---|
| **NEVER EVER** | **ALMOST NEVER** | **SOME- TIMES** | **ALMOST ALWAYS** | **ALWAYS** |

_____ 16. I become frustrated when I have to wait for the teacher to finish giving directions.

| 1 | 2 | 3 | 4 | 5 |
|---|---|---|---|---|
| **NEVER EVER** | **ALMOST NEVER** | **SOME- TIMES** | **ALMOST ALWAYS** | **ALWAYS** |

_____ 17. I prefer to build things by myself without anyone's guidance.

| 1 | 2 | 3 | 4 | 5 |
|---|---|---|---|---|
| **NEVER EVER** | **ALMOST NEVER** | **SOME- TIMES** | **ALMOST ALWAYS** | **ALWAYS** |

_____ 18. I become frustrated if directions are changed while I am working on the assignment.

| 1 | 2 | 3 | 4 | 5 |
|---|---|---|---|---|
| **NEVER EVER** | **ALMOST NEVER** | **SOME- TIMES** | **ALMOST ALWAYS** | **ALWAYS** |

_____ 19. I keep detailed notes so I have the right answers for tests.

| 1 | 2 | 3 | 4 | 5 |
|---|---|---|---|---|
| **NEVER EVER** | **ALMOST NEVER** | **SOME- TIMES** | **ALMOST ALWAYS** | **ALWAYS** |

_____ 20. I don't like having to do my work in the way the teacher says, especially when I have a better idea I would like to try.

| 1 | 2 | 3 | 4 | 5 |
|---|---|---|---|---|
| **NEVER EVER** | **ALMOST NEVER** | **SOME- TIMES** | **ALMOST ALWAYS** | **ALWAYS** |

_____ 21. I clean up my work area and put things back where they belong without being told to do so.

| 1 | 2 | 3 | 4 | 5 |
|---|---|---|---|---|
| **NEVER EVER** | **ALMOST NEVER** | **SOME- TIMES** | **ALMOST ALWAYS** | **ALWAYS** |

_____ 22. I enjoy the challenge of fixing or building something.

| 1 | 2 | 3 | 4 | 5 |
|---|---|---|---|---|
| **NEVER EVER** | **ALMOST NEVER** | **SOME-TIMES** | **ALMOST ALWAYS** | **ALWAYS** |

_____ 23. I react quickly to assignments and questions without thinking through my answers.

| 1 | 2 | 3 | 4 | 5 |
|---|---|---|---|---|
| **NEVER EVER** | **ALMOST NEVER** | **SOME-TIMES** | **ALMOST ALWAYS** | **ALWAYS** |

_____ 24. I enjoy researching and writing factual reports.

| 1 | 2 | 3 | 4 | 5 |
|---|---|---|---|---|
| **NEVER EVER** | **ALMOST NEVER** | **SOME-TIMES** | **ALMOST ALWAYS** | **ALWAYS** |

_____ 25. I ask more questions than most people because I just enjoy knowing things.

| 1 | 2 | 3 | 4 | 5 |
|---|---|---|---|---|
| **NEVER EVER** | **ALMOST NEVER** | **SOME-TIMES** | **ALMOST ALWAYS** | **ALWAYS** |

_____ 26. I like to figure out how things work.

| 1 | 2 | 3 | 4 | 5 |
|---|---|---|---|---|
| **NEVER EVER** | **ALMOST NEVER** | **SOME-TIMES** | **ALMOST ALWAYS** | **ALWAYS** |

_____ 27. I am told by others that I am very organized.

| 1 | 2 | 3 | 4 | 5 |
|---|---|---|---|---|
| **NEVER EVER** | **ALMOST NEVER** | **SOME-TIMES** | **ALMOST ALWAYS** | **ALWAYS** |

_____ 28. I like to make up my own way of doing things.

| 1 | 2 | 3 | 4 | 5 |
|---|---|---|---|---|
| **NEVER EVER** | **ALMOST NEVER** | **SOME-TIMES** | **ALMOST ALWAYS** | **ALWAYS** |

Part II: Please answer each of the following questions in your own words.

What makes assignments frustrating for you?

If you could choose, what
would you do to show your
teacher what you have learned?

If you were the teacher, how
would you have students learn?

# SCORING SHEET

Name_____ Teacher_____

Write the number of your response in the center of the tumbler under the appropriate question number. Add up the tumbler numbers and write the total in the space at the end of each line. Then transfer your total for each scheme to the bar graph at the bottom of the page.

| Schema | 2 | 5 | 10 | 13 | 18 | 21 | 27 | TOTAL |
|---|---|---|---|---|---|---|---|---|
| **Sequential Processor** | ⊛ | ⊛ | ⊛ | ⊛ | ⊛ | ⊛ | ⊛ | _____ |
| | 4 | 7 | 9 | 14 | 19 | 24 | 25 | |
| **Precise Processor** | ⊛ | ⊛ | ⊛ | ⊛ | ⊛ | ⊛ | ⊛ | _____ |
| | 1 | 6 | 11 | 15 | 17 | 22 | 26 | |
| **Technical Processor** | ⊛ | ⊛ | ⊛ | ⊛ | ⊛ | ⊛ | ⊛ | _____ |
| | 3 | 8 | 12 | 16 | 20 | 23 | 28 | |
| **Confluent Processor** | ⊛ | ⊛ | ⊛ | ⊛ | ⊛ | ⊛ | ⊛ | _____ |

## Your Learning Combination

Graph the totals from each of the tumbler lines above on the appropriate bars below.

| SCHEMA | I avoid this scheme. | I use this as needed. | I use this scheme first. |
|---|---|---|---|
| | 7       12 | 17     21     25 | 30       35 |
| **Sequential Processor** | ▶ □□□□□□□□□ | □□□□□□□□□ | □□□□□□□□□ |
| **Precise Processor** | ▶ □□□□□□□□□ | □□□□□□□□□ | □□□□□□□□□ |
| **Technical Processor** | ▶ □□□□□□□□□ | □□□□□□□□□ | □□□□□□□□□ |
| **Confluent Processor** | ▶ □□□□□□□□□ | □□□□□□□□□ | □□□□□□□□□ |

The following written expressions are representative of each of the four learning schemas. As you read the written responses on the Learning Combination Inventory, look for similarities in words, meaning, or intent with the learning schema identifiers listed below. Record the classification next to each written response and then see if the respondent's written section matches his or her schema preferences on the Scoring Sheet.

| Sequential Processor | Precise Processor | Technical Processor | Confluent Processor |
|---|---|---|---|
| | | *Technical Reasoning/ Hands On* | |
| *Clear Directions* | *Correct Information* | | *Use My Own Ideas* |
| I become frustrated when the directions aren't clear or don't make sense. | I want to know all the answers; I want to know what will be on the test. | I want hands-on activities that interest me instead of taking notes, doing book work, or writing about it. | I am frustrated when I feel trapped in the teacher's ideas. That's when I don't even feel like doing the assignment. |
| I don't work well when I don't have good instructions or the teacher doesn't do a good job of explaining the assignment. | I like the teacher to see that my work is correct. I'm frustrated when I don't know all the answers because I like doing the work right so that I get a good grade. | Give me the tools and let me demonstrate what I know hands-on. Let me build things! | I am frustrated when I come up with a certain idea and I'm not allowed to use it. I don't like it when teachers don't let you use your own ideas. |
| I hate it when the teacher keeps changing the directions in the middle of the assignment. | I am frustrated when I don't have enough information or I can't find the information and the answers aren't in the book. | Give me a real challenging project with a point to it and let me figure it out. *Autonomy/Outside* | I don't like having to do an assignment in one certain way. |
| *Practice/Planning* | *Detailed Information* | I need to run around outside and get things to make sense in my head. | I don't like following lots of rules and regulations. |
| It's hard when the teacher isn't organized or doesn't explain things thoroughly. I want the teacher to go over and over the assignment until I understand it. | I become frustrated when the teacher doesn't go into detail and explain things. Confusion! I would have students take notes and do activities to reinforce the information. | Let students have more breaks during the day to go outside. Let me learn by going home and living and experiencing it. | *Use of Imagination* I like to use my imagination. Let students learn however they want. |
| I like the teacher to go slow and make sure everybody is at the same spot. | I like trivia. I'm good at that. | Let students learn however they want. | I like exploring new things. I like to work with people who are curious and don't do assignments in just one way. |
| I always practice my answers by going over and over them. | I take detailed notes and then go over and over them. | I don't let the teacher know what I know. I am a very private person. I keep it inside. | I like learning in a creative, fun, entertaining way. |
| I like plenty of in-class practice. | | I don't want to show a teacher what I know. I'm happy the way I am. | I like coming up with artistic and crafty things. |

| Sequential Processor | Precise Processor | Technical Processor | Confluent Processor |
| --- | --- | --- | --- |
| Time to Complete Work<br><br>I need time to study and to complete the work in class.<br><br>I'm frustrated when the teacher gives us lots of worksheets and no time to do the work and go over it in class.<br><br>I don't like it when I don't have enough time to do a thorough job<br><br>Neat/Double-Checked<br><br>I need time to make my work look neat and to make sure my answers are correct<br><br>I don't want my work to look sloppy so I need time to do the work neatly. | Asking/Answering *Questions*<br><br>I like to show people what I know by *answering all the* teacher's questions.<br><br>I like to take tests and quizzes to show what I know.<br><br>If you want to know what I know, read my answers or ask me questions.<br><br>*Writing Detailed Answers*<br><br>I have a better voice when I am writing than when I am speaking publicly.<br><br>I like to show what I know by writing a several-page paper and looking stuff up. | Let me work at home where there is no one to bother me.<br><br>*Real-World Experiences*<br><br>I learn better from real-world experiences.<br><br>Take me out into the real world and show me something.<br><br>I learn by living what I learn.<br><br>I learn better if I can do what I am learning about. | I like to do storytelling where you use pictures and your own imagination.<br><br>*Presentations/Creative Writing*<br><br>I like to write things the same way I'd say them.<br><br>I like writing stories using my own ideas and not some dumb book.<br><br>I like to stand up and talk.<br><br>I like to express myself through oral presentations, skits, and creative projects |

# Appendix B
# Learning Combination Lock Manipulative

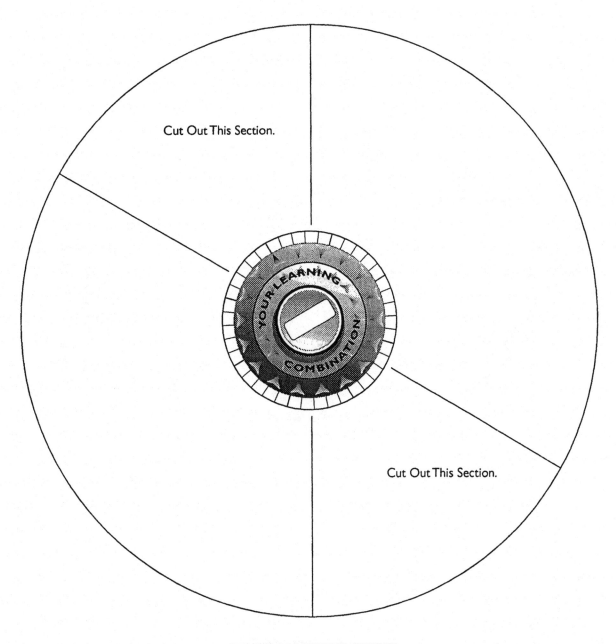

Cut Out This Section.

Cut Out This Section.

**LOCK MANIPULATIVE**

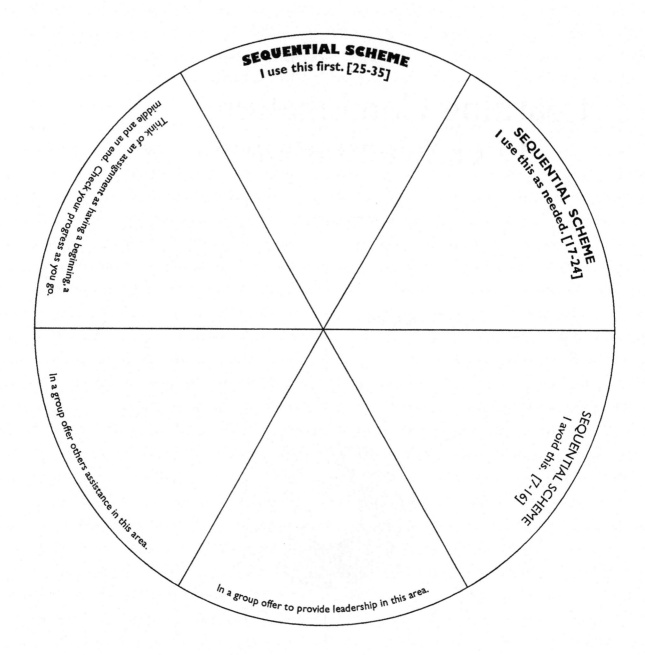

**SEQUENTIAL SCHEME**
I use this first. [25-35]

**SEQUENTIAL SCHEME**
I use this as needed. [17-24]

SEQUENTIAL SCHEME
I avoid this. [7-16]

In a group offer to provide leadership in this area.

In a group offer others assistance in this area.

Think of an assignment as having a beginning, a middle and an end. Check your progress as you go.

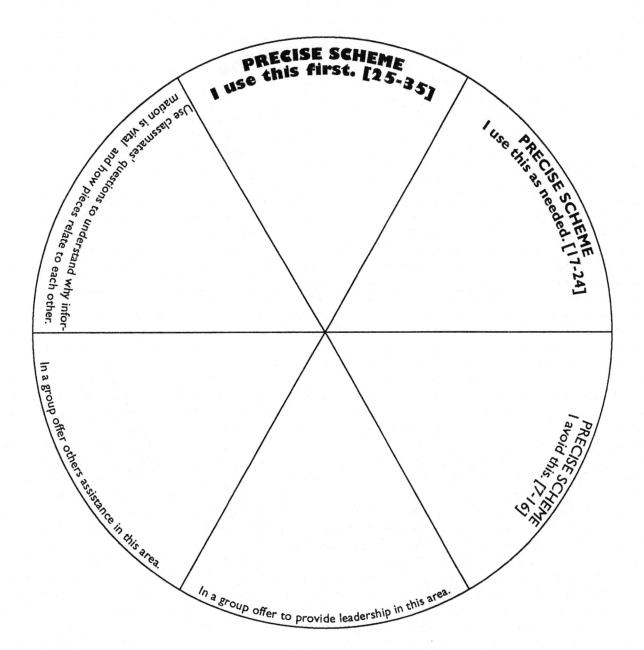

PRECISE SCHEME
I use this first. [25-35]

PRECISE SCHEME
I use this as needed. [17-24]

PRECISE SCHEME
I avoid this. [7-16]

Use classmates' questions to understand why information is vital and how pieces relate to each other.

In a group offer others assistance in this area.

In a group offer to provide leadership in this area.

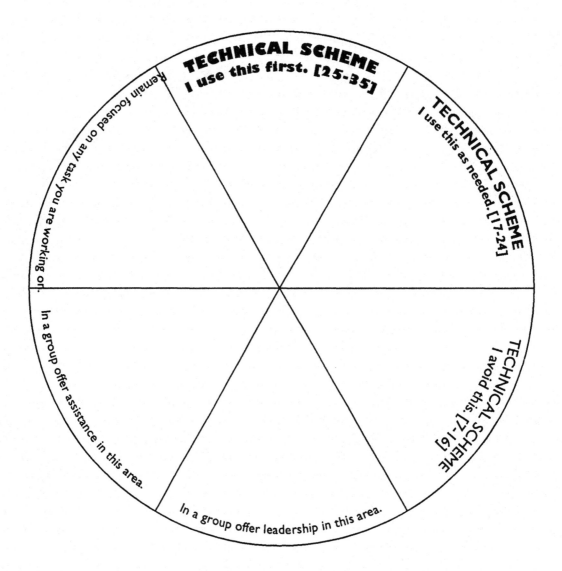

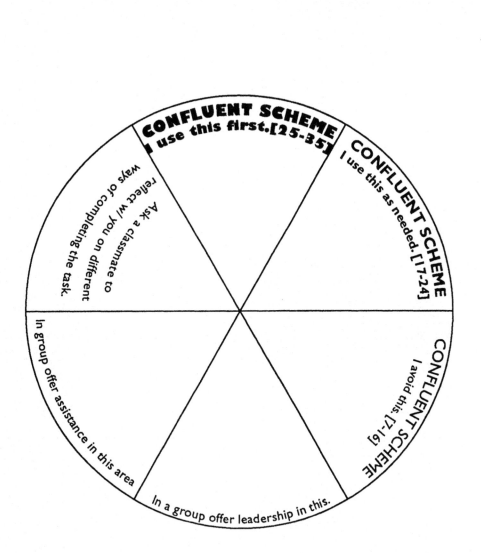

# References

Ach, N. (1935). Analyse des willens [Analysis of will]. In E. Abderholden (Ed.), *Handbuch der biologische arbeiten methoden* [Handbook of biological work methods] (Vol. 6). Berlin: Urban & Schwarzenberg.

Allport, G. (1961). *Pattern and growth in personality.* New York: Holt, Rinehart & Winston.

Assagioli, R. (1973). *The act of will.* New York: Viking.

Atkinson, J., & Birch, D. (1970). *The dynamics of action.* New York: John Wiley.

Bandura, A. (1977). Self-efficacy: Toward a unifying theory of behavioral changes. *Psychological Review, 84,* 191-215.

Barna, G. (1992). *The power of vision.* Ventura, CA: Regal Books.

Barrett, B. (1931). *Strength of will and how to develop it.* New York: Ruland B. Smith.

Blowe, P. (1995). Unpublished reflective journal entry, Rowan College of New Jersey, Glassboro.

Boyer, E. (1993, May 5). *School reform in perspective.* Invited address presented at the Rowan Distinguished Scholar Series, Rowan College of New Jersey, Glassboro.

Brophy, J. (1987). Synthesis of research on strategies for motivating students to learn. *Educational Leadership, 45*(2), 40-48.

Brown, B. K. (1995). Unpublished teaching platform, Rowan College of New Jersey, Glassboro.

Bruner, J. (1960). *The process of education.* Cambridge, MA: Harvard University Press.

Caine, R., & Caine, G. (1991). *Making connections: Teaching and the human brain.* Alexandria, VA: ASCD.

Callahan, R. (1962). *Education and the cult of efficiency.* Chicago: University of Chicago Press.

Cannon, A., & Greve, F. (1995, June 9). Pilot's survival no surprise to family, friends. *Philadelphia Inquirer,* pp. 1, 16.

de Chardin, P. T. (1959). *Le phenomene humaine* [The phenomenon of man] (with introduction by J. Huxley; B. Wall, Trans.). New York: Harper & Row. (Original work published 1923)

Dexter, C. (1994). *The daughters of Cain.* London: Macmillan.

Duncan, R. (1991, April 18-20). *An examination of Vygotsky's theory of children's private speech.* Paper presented at the meeting of the Society for Research in Child Development, Seattle, WA.

Dweck, C. (1986). Motivational processes affecting learning. *American Psychologist, 41*(10), 1040-1048.

Elkind, D. (1981). *The hurried child, growing up too fast too soon.* Reading, MA: Addison-Wesley.

Elliott, P. (1986). Right (or left) brain cognition, wrong metaphor for creative behavior: It is prefrontal lobe volition that makes the difference in the release of creative potential. *Journal of Creative Behavior, 20*(3), 202-214.

Ellis, S., & Whalen, S. (1992). Keys to cooperative learning. *Instructor, 2,* 34-37.

Evans, J. (1995). Unpublished teaching platform, Rowan College of New Jersey, Glassboro.

Falkowski, C. (1995). Unpublished reflective journal entry, Rowan College of New Jersey, Glassboro.

Fenstermacher, G. (1990). Some considerations on teaching as a moral profession. In J. Goodlad, R. Soder, & K. Sirotnik (Eds.), *The moral dimensions of teaching.* San Francisco: Jossey-Bass.

Ferrell, B. (1983). A factor analytic comparison of four learning styles instruments. *Journal of Educational Psychology, 75*(1), 33-39.

Flavell, J. (1980, Fall). A tribute to Piaget. *Society for Research in Child Development Newsletter,* 1.

Fullan, M. (1991). *The new meaning of educational change* (2nd ed.). New York: Teachers College Press.

Gammons, P. (1990, April 30). Forever a kid: Robin Yount has MVP talents worth millions but revels in high risk fun with big toys. *Sports Illustrated, 72*(18), 76-92.

Gardner, H. (1983). *Frames of mind: The theory of multiple intelligences.* New York: Basic Books.

Gardner, H. (1989). Beyond a modular view of mind. In W. Damon (Ed.), *Child development today and tomorrow.* San Francisco: Jossey-Bass.

Gholar, C., Givens, S., McPherson, M., & Riggs, E. (1991, April). *Wellness begins when the child comes first: The relationship between the conative domain and the school achievement paradigm.* Paper presented at the annual convention of the American Association for Counseling and Development, Reno, NV.

Ginott, H. (1972). *Teacher and child: A book for parents and teachers.* New York: Macmillan.

Gleick, J. (1987). *Chaos: Making a new science.* New York: Viking.

Glickman, C. (1991). Pretending not to know that we know. *Educational Leadership, 48*(4), 4-10.

Greenspan, S., & Lodish, R. (1991). School literacy: The real ABC's. *Phi Delta Kappan, 73*(4), 300-308.

Gregorc, A., & Ward, H. (1977). A new definition for individual. *NASSP, 61*(406), 20-26.

Hershberger, W. A. (Ed.). (1989). *Volitional action: Conation and control.* Amsterdam: Elsevier Science.

Hilgard, E. (1980). The trilogy of the mind: Cognition, affectation and conation. *Journal of the History of the Behavioral Sciences, 16,* 107-117.

James, P. D. (1986). *A taste for death.* New York: Warner Books.

James, P. D. (1988). *Shroud for a nightingale.* New York: Warner Books.

James, W. (1904). *Talks to teachers on psychology: And to students on some of life's ideals.* New York: Norton.

Johnston, C. (1993, August). *A request for funding: Unlocking the will to learn.* Unpublished proposal, Rowan College of New Jersey, Glassboro.

Johnston, C. (1994a). *Empowering the organization through professional talk.* Dubuque, IA: Kendall-Hunt.

Johnston, C. (1994b, September). *The interactive learning model.* Paper presented at the meeting of the British Education Research Association, Oxford University, Queen Anne's College, Oxford, UK.

Johnston. C. (1995, September). *Dimensions of the interactive learning model.* Paper presented at the European Conference on Educational Research, University of Bath, Bath, UK.

Johnston, C. (1996, April 17). *Many voices—one message: A cross-cultural study of student learning processes with implications for students, teachers and reformers.* Paper presented at the International Symposium on Economics, Cultures, Communities, and Schools: Finding the Connection, Examining the Alternatives, Rowan College of New Jersey, Glassboro.

Johnston, C., & Dainton, G. (1994a, April). *Cooperative learning: Synergy, chaos or inertia.* Paper presented at the annual meeting of the American Educational Research Association, New Orleans, LA.

Johnston, C., & Dainton, G. (1994b). Death by classroom: The perpetrator and the victims. In J. Rowan (Ed.), *Occasional papers on collaboration in education.* Vineland, NJ: Standard.

Jung, C. (1923). *Psychological types* (H. G. Baynes, Trans.). New York: Harcourt Brace.

Kahler, T. (1977). The miniscript. In G. Barnes (Ed.), *Transactional analysis after Eric Berne.* New York: Harper & Row.

Kant, I. (1888). *The philosophy of Kant as contained in extracts from his own writings* (J. Watson, Trans.). Glasgow, UK: Maclehose & Jackson.

Keefe, J. (1992). Thinking about the thinking movement. In J. Keefe & H. Walberg (Eds.), *Teaching for thinking.* Reston, VA: NASSP.

Keefe, J., & Ferrell, B. (1990). Developing a defensible learning style paradigm. *Educational Leadership, 48*(2), 57-61.

Keefe, J., & Languis, M. (1983, October). *Operational definitions.* Paper presented to the NASSP Learning Styles Task Force, Reston, VA.

Kolb, D. (1984)). *Experiential learning: Experience as the source of learning and development.* Englewood Cliffs, NJ: Prentice Hall.

Kuhl, J. (1986). Motivation and information processing: A new look at decision making, dynamic conflict, and action control. In R. N. Sorrentino & E. T. Higgins (Eds.), *The handbook of motivation and cognition: Foundation of social behavior.* New York: Guilford.

Lattimore, R. (Trans.). (1965). *The odyssey of Homer.* New York: Harper & Row.

Levin, B. (1994). Putting students at the center. *Phi Delta Kappan, 75,* 758-760.

MacLean, P. (1978). A mind of three minds: Educating the triune brain. In *The 77th yearbook of the National Society for the Study of Education.* Chicago: University of Chicago Press.

Masters, E. (1992). *Spoon River anthology: An annotated edition* (J. E. Hallwas, Ed.). Urbana: University of Illinois Press. (Original work published 1915)

May, R. (1969). *Love and will.* New York: Norton.

McFarland, C. (1992). Cooperative learning shows staying power. *ASCD Update, 34*(3), 2.

Myers, I., & Briggs, K. (1976). *Myers-Briggs type indicator.* Palo Alto, CA: Consulting Psychologist Press.

Palonsky, S. (1986). *900 shows a year: A look at teaching from a teacher's side of the desk.* New York: Random House.

Pay, R. (1981). Control of complex conation and emotion in the neocortex by the limbic entorhinal, subicular, and cingulate cortexes and the hypothalamus, mammillary body, and thalamus. *International Journal of Neuroscience, 15,* 1-30.

Pears, D. (Ed.). (1963). *Freedom and the will.* London: Macmillan.

Peterson, P. (1982). Beyond time on task: Student's reports of their thought processes during direct instruction. *Elementary School Journal, 82,* 481-491.

Philip, H. (1936). *An experimental study of the frustration of will-acts and conation.* Cambridge, UK: Cambridge University Press.

Piaget, J. (1952). *The origins of intelligence in children* (M. Cook, Trans.). New York: International Universities Press.

Postman, N. (1979). *Teaching as a conserving activity.* New York: Dell.

Powers, W. (1989). Volition: A semi-scientific essay. In W. A. Hershberger (Ed.), *Volitional action: Conation and control.* Amsterdam: Elsevier Science.

Redding, N. (1990). Empowering learners project. *Educational Leadership, 47*(5), 46-48.

Reissman, F. (1964). The strategy of style. *Teachers College Record, 65,* 484-489.

*Report of the management science panel on principal certification.* (1989). Trenton: State of New Jersey.

Sallstrom, P. (1991). The essence of dialogue. In B. Goranzon & M. Florin (Eds.), *Dialogue and technology: Culture and knowledge.* Berlin: Springer-Verlag.

Sander, F. (1930). Structure, totality of experience, and gestalt. *Psychologie, 202.*

Santrouck, J. (1994). *Child development.* Dubuque, IA: William C. Brown.

Satir, V. (1972). *Peoplemaking.* Palo Alto, CA: Science and Behavior Books.

Schiefele, U., & Csikszentmihalyi, M. (1994). Interest and the quality of experience in the classroom. *European Journal of Psychology of Education, 9*(3), 251-270.

Schmeck, R. (1988). Strategies and styles of learning: An integration of varied perspectives. In R. Schmeck (Ed.), *Learning strategies and learning styles.* New York: Plenum.

Skinner, B. (1989). The origins of cognitive thought. *American Psychologist, 44*(1), 13-18.

Slavin, R. (1980). Cooperative learning. *Review of Educational Research, 50,* 315-342.

Smith, F. (1995). Let's declare education a disaster and get on with our lives. *Phi Delta Kappan, 76*(8), 584-590.

Snow, R., & Jackson, D. (1992). *Assessment of conative constructs for educational research and evaluation: A catalogue.* Washington, DC: U.S. Department of Education, Office of Educational Research and Improvement.

Tempte, T. (1991). The chair of Tutankhamen (S. Robertson, Trans.). In B. Goranzon & M. Florin (Eds.), *Dialogue and technology: Culture and knowledge.* Berlin: Springer-Verlag.

Thompson, D. (1961). *On growth and form* (J. T. Bonner, Ed.). Cambridge, UK: Cambridge University Press.

Thoreau, H. (1963). *The variorum drummer* (W. Harding, Ed.). New York: Washington Square Press.

Vygotsky, L. (1962). *Thought and language.* Cambridge: MIT Press.

*Webster's ninth new collegiate dictionary.* (1991). Springfield, MA: Merriam-Webster.

Whitehead, A. (1929). *Aims of education.* New York: Macmillan.

Winne, P., & Marx, R. (1980). Matching student's cognitive responses to teaching skills. *Journal of Educational Psychology, 72,* 257-264.

Witkin, H. (1978). *Field-dependence in personal and cultural adaptation.* Worcester, MA: Clark University Press.

Witkin, H., & Goodenough, D. (1982). Cognitive styles: Essence and origins. *Psychological Issue, Monograph 51.*

Wittrock, M. (1994). Students' thought processes. In M. Wittrock (Ed.), *Handbook of research on teaching* (4th ed.). New York: Macmillan.

Yellin, D., & Blake, M. (1994). *Integrating the language arts.* New York: HarperCollins.

Zimmerman, B., & Martinez-Pons, M. (1988). Construct validation of a strategy model of student self-regulated learning. *Journal of Educational Psychology, 80*(3), 284-290.

# Index

CORWIN
PRESS

**The Corwin Press logo**—a raven striding across an open book—represents the happy union of courage and learning. We are a professional-level publisher of books and journals for K-12 educators, and we are committed to creating and providing resources that embody these qualities. Corwin's motto is "Success for All Learners."

CPSIA information can be obtained
at www.ICGtesting.com
Printed in the USA
FSOW04n1634291015
12751FS

9 780803 963924